The Letort Papers

SOME OF THE BEST WEAPONS FOR COUNTERINSURGENTS DO NOT SHOOT

Eric T. Olson

October 2010

*****

Comments pertaining to this report are invited and should be forwarded to: Director, Strategic Studies Institute, U.S. Army War College, 122 Forbes Ave, Carlisle, PA 17013-5244.

*****

All Strategic Studies Institute (SSI) publications may be downloaded free of charge from the SSI website. Hard copies of this report may also be obtained free of charge by placing an order on the SSI website. The SSI website address is: *www.StrategicStudiesInstitute.army.mil*.

*****

The Strategic Studies Institute publishes a monthly e-mail newsletter to update the national security community on the research of our analysts, recent and forthcoming publications, and upcoming conferences sponsored by the Institute. Each newsletter also provides a strategic commentary by one of our research analysts. If you are interested in receiving this newsletter, please subscribe on the SSI website at *www.StrategicStudiesInstitute. army.mil/newsletter/*.

ISBN 1-58487-466-x

CONTENTS

FOREWORD

The American military's attitude towards reconstruction has been ambivalent, to say the least. In the aftermath of World War II, the successful rebuilding of Western Europe that was the result of the carefully crafted and skillfully executed Marshall Plan was one of the most significant achievements of the 20th century. But in the wake of the Vietnam experience, reconstruction became an undertaking to be avoided at almost any cost. "Nation building" became a pejorative expression in the lexicon of the military and policymakers.

All that seems to have changed since the attacks of September 11, 2001. The experience on the ground gained by Army forces in two major counterinsurgency operations has proved that reconstruction designed to win the support of a population away from the enemy is an integral part of a successful counterinsurgency strategy. The publication of new Army doctrine followed and codified this reshaping of our thinking about reconstruction and its relationship to counterinsurgency warfare.

But the matter of maximizing the effectiveness of a reconstruction effort undertaken as part of a counterinsurgency campaign is still very much at issue. It is not clear from our doctrine that we really have a clear concept for how to undertake reconstruction, nor do we have a common understanding across the force of what its component activities are, who should be responsible for them, or what specific capabilities need to be resident in our Army units to accomplish the necessary component tasks.

In this monograph, Eric T. Olson first provides some historical context, tracking the role that reconstruction has played in military operations from the War in the Philippines to the conflicts that are ongoing today. This is followed by a doctrinal treatment that lays the ground work for an analysis of how we think about reconstruction, the way that we execute it, and the challenges that we face in doing so. Mr. Olson concludes his discussion with recommendations for enhancing the Army's ability to realize the full potential of reconstruction as a critical contributing factor in a larger counterinsurgency campaign.

There seems to be no end in sight to the long war in which the Army currently finds itself taking part. To the degree that battles of this war will be fought as counterinsurgencies, this monograph establishes an important starting point for discussions about how to conduct the campaign more effectively.

DOUGLAS C. LOVELACE, JR.
Director
Strategic Studies Institute

ABOUT THE AUTHOR

ERIC T. OLSON, was the Deputy Director of the Iraq Reconstruction Management Office, Civil-Military Affairs in the U.S. Embassy, Baghdad from 2006-07. Following that, from 2007-08 he served as the Chief of Staff and Principal Advisor to the Special Inspector General for Iraq Reconstruction. An Army officer for 34 years, he commanded infantry units at all levels from platoon to division, achieving the rank of major general and serving his last 3 years as the Commanding General of the 25th Infantry Division (Light), which included duty as the Commander of Combined Joint Task Force-76, during Operation ENDURING FREEDOM in Afghanistan (2004-05).

SUMMARY

If the U.S. Army's current experience in ongoing overseas operations like those in Iraq and Afghanistan are any indication, reconstruction has become an integral part of the American way of war. And judging from the disappointing results of reconstruction efforts in these operations, measured mostly in terms of the effect that such efforts have had on the course of these wars, there is much lacking in the Army's understanding of reconstruction itself and the role that it will likely play in all future operations, especially in counterinsurgencies (COIN).

Reconstruction is defined in current Army doctrine as "the process of rebuilding degraded, damaged, or destroyed political, socioeconomic, and physical infrastructure of a country or territory to create the foundation for long-term development." The term itself has been used in the recounting of the history of U.S. warfare for quite some time, most notably first applied to the period of rebuilding after the Civil War. The Marshall Plan and associated activities that took place in Europe and Japan in the wake of World War II represent reconstruction's finest hour.

But it is only recently that reconstruction has been viewed as an integral part of operations that are under way as opposed to some sort of post-conflict or post-crisis activity. During the U.S. invasion and subsequent occupation of the Philippines at the turn of the 20th century, Brigadier General James F. Smith used the term "benevolent assimilation" to describe his approach to winning over the population as he battled rebel forces in the subdistrict of Negros. His view was that securing the population and taking action to establish good governance and stability and address the pressing basic needs of the people were perhaps more important than combat operations against the insurgents with whom his forces were engaged. But despite the demonstrated success of this approach in America's "small wars" of the 20th century, embracing reconstruction as an essential part of warfare has been the exception as opposed to the rule. Often decried as "nation building," reconstruction more often than not has been viewed as an activity to be avoided—a mission that would undermine the primary role of U.S. forces as "warfighters."

Recently published doctrine for U.S. forces sends the strong signal that the U.S. Army is unequivocally in the business of nation-building if we are to prosecute successful COIN campaigns. *Field Manual (FM) 3-0, Operations,* includes a discussion of reconstruction as inextricably linked to counterinsurgency—a form of irregular warfare that is one of the manual's operational themes. In *Field Manual (FM) 3-07, Stability Operations*, the term reconstruction is defined for the first time ever in U.S. Army doctrine and discussed extensively throughout the manual. But it is in *Field Manual (FM) 3-24, Counterinsurgency*, that the importance, if not preeminence, of reconstruction is most clearly stated, captured explicitly in the observation in the manual that "some of the best weapons for counterinsurgents do not shoot."[1]

That said, descriptions of reconstruction in Army doctrine fall short on several counts. First, there is still some conceptual confusion in the definition of reconstruction and its further specification that the new doctrine presumably was meant to clear up. The treatment of reconstruction in the manuals includes discussion of an overwhelming number of tasks and, raises questions about prioritization and responsibilities for their accomplishment. Most critically, none of the manuals includes a description of a concept of reconstruction, thereby leaving a void for commanders in the field who are seeking guidelines for the integration of reconstruction with other activities that are associated with COIN.

Working from the assumption that some of the shortcomings of Army doctrine are being compensated for by practitioners in current operations, a simple tabletop exercise was conducted in the Spring of 2009 to examine how reconstruction is presently being executed as part of COIN. Participants were solicited based on their knowledge of and experience in the key agencies involved in past and likely future reconstruction operations. To generate feedback from player agencies, a base scenario was designed that described conditions in a nation typical of those found by U.S. forces in recent and ongoing overseas operations, and which are likely to be similar to those that will be encountered during future operations. The results of the exercise demonstrate that there is little disagreement among the key players in reconstruction operations about what the critical tasks are or even how to prioritize them, but that there *is* a need for some articulation of how to organize and coordinate reconstruction operations beyond what exists now in doctrine or applicable governmental directives.

Establishing an agreed upon framework for reconstruction in COIN which is accepted by the participating agencies will go a long way toward addressing the shortcomings, conceptual confusion, and missing clarity that has characterized such efforts to date. A concept of reconstruction that is constructed along the same lines as other operational concepts that are prevalent in Army doctrine would provide such a framework. Such an operational concept might include as components a statement of the purpose of reconstruction, a description of its essential elements, a general sequence and scheme of reconstruction activities, and guidelines for assigning responsibilities and assessment of a reconstruction effort.

Once such a framework is in place and the role of key players is more clearly established, it will be important for the Army to look for ways to make reconstruction a more effective component of its counterinsurgency operations—both to increase the likelihood of successful campaigns and to reduce some of the toll that counterinsurgency campaigns are taking on our servicemen and women.

There are some fundamental reforms that must be considered that could add significantly to Army capabilities to conduct reconstruction. Some of these involve interagency reforms, the most important being a shared understanding of a reconstruction concept across agencies, roles and responsibilities that are more appropriately assigned to and accepted by them, and an enhanced operational focus in those agencies which are instrumental to reconstruction that would allow them to deploy in greater numbers earlier on in a campaign. But the Army as a key player in reconstruction as part of COIN, must reexamine its capabilities to participate in a broad interagency effort, or to act alone when that seems appropriate or necessary.

Some areas that will need to be addressed are the current approach to training and otherwise preparing for reconstruction in counterinsurgency operations, the adequacy of capabilities that are currently resident in Army units to execute key reconstruction, and the Army's current ability and approach to setting conditions for the success of its interagency partners.

Even under the best circumstances, reconstruction in COIN is a difficult endeavor. The most critical tasks are numerous and complex. Many participating agencies must undertake missions that fall well out of their existing core competencies or operate in environments that are completely unfamiliar to them. The involvement of multiple agencies which are not accustomed to working together makes coordination difficult. And all this must take place in an environment where an armed, violent foe understands the disadvantage to him of a successful reconstruction effort and is determined to go to almost any length to resist progress or destroy what has been accomplished.

In an assessment of an ongoing counterinsurgency operation, General David H. Petraeus observed that "hard is not hopeless."[2] Extending this logic, it can be said that reconstruction in COIN is hard, but it becomes less hopeless if the counterinsurgent understands what needs to be accomplished and to what end, and he has a plan and can mount a coordinated effort to execute that plan. If so executed, reconstruction can indeed become one of the array of key weapons that do not shoot available to the counterinsurgent.

But even as a weapon that does not shoot, reconstruction can end up being dangerous to the hunter as well as the hunted. The counterinsurgent's ultimate objectives are a manageable security environment and strong national institutions that have the confidence and the support of the people. A coordinated, skillfully executed reconstruction program is essential to those ends. But reconstruction that is mismanaged, bungled, and obviously ineffectual not only represents a lost opportunity to advance the cause; it also may well put a weapon in the hands of the insurgent.

ENDNOTES - SUMMARY

1. *Field Manual (FM) 3-24/Marine Corps Warfighting Publication (MCWP) 3-33.5, Counterinsurgency*, Washington, DC: Department of the Army, para. 1-153.

2. See for example, General David Petraeus, quoted by Josh Partlow in "Path in Iraq Hard But Not Hopeless, US General Says," *The Washington Post*, February 11, 2007.

CHAPTER 1

INTRODUCTION

In the summer of 2006, violence in Iraq was at near record highs, and pressure from Washington to show some progress in reducing it was mounting. Though there were some reasons for hope based on developments in the outlying provinces (for example, early signs of the Sunni awakening were being recognized), the situation in Baghdad seemed to get worse every day. The U.S. Ambassador to Iraq and the Force Commander of the Multinational Force decided that a change in strategy was necessary. Whereas to this point the approach had been to be strong in as many places as possible throughout Iraq and focus on turning provinces over to Iraqi control as soon as conditions allowed, the Force Commander decided that a reduction in violence throughout Iraq had to begin in Baghdad, the capital city with one-quarter of the nation's population. There, violence was raging unabated, and an all out civil war on top of an already well-established, stubborn insurgency was seen as a real possibility. This campaign to stabilize Iraq's most important metropolitan center became known the "Baghdad Security Plan."

As the heart of the Baghdad-focused strategy, a classic counterinsurgency (COIN) approach was adopted by tactical units in the neighborhoods, which became known by the mnemonic "clear, hold, build." The first step was to clear neighborhoods of insurgent activity and the influence of sectarian extremists primarily by using U.S. forces to conduct combat operations against insurgent groups and violent militias. The "hold phase" came next, with emphasis on main-

1

taining security and stability in neighborhoods, using Iraqi security forces wherever possible to accomplish the task. Once the neighborhood was secured, the critical "build phase" was to begin. The concept was to redouble efforts to undertake reconstruction projects, focused especially on putting unemployed military-aged males to work and restoring essential services to the neighborhoods, but also to work with the local population and government to strengthen institutions and build capacity—reestablish the rule of law, improve governance, rekindle economic and commercial activity, reopen banks and medical centers, and the like. The outcome of the build phase was viewed as decisive. By establishing a sense of normalcy in the local population, one that would convince them that life would be much better if the neighborhood were kept under the control of legitimate government authorities and away from the influence of the insurgents, a successful build phase could make the hold phase a less daunting task for security forces in the neighborhoods.

The strategy was sound, and the clear phase commenced with significant early success. Coalition forces arriving in Baghdad and its bordering provinces began to push out into neighborhoods that had previously been considered firmly in the grip of various insurgent and extremist groups—Al Qaeda in Iraq, Sunni rejectionists, Shia militants, and several others.

But the campaign's hold and build phases as originally conceived are broadly judged to have failed. While U.S. forces were committed to clearing neighborhoods, Iraqi Army and National Police forces were not equal to the task of securing them, meaning that clearing forces often had to return to neighborhoods or simply remain there in order to hold onto security gains that had been so hard won.

This inability to hold was complicated by the fact that the build phase floundered. Naturally, building proved difficult in neighborhoods where instability threatened. But it was not just a lack of security that explains the failure to mount any significant reconstruction effort. Fundamental weaknesses in the planning and execution of the reconstruction effort in support of the Baghdad Security Plan were crippling. To begin with, there was no reconstruction master plan for Baghdad that was agreed to by those members of the interagency community who had a reconstruction mission and capabilities to carry it out. A clear, shared vision of the purpose of reconstruction as it related to the campaign was lacking. The effort was marked by disorganization that was endemic throughout, and there was a noticeable lack of coordination between reconstruction agencies and organizations. There was little to no integration of the various reconstruction efforts and the military operations of forces that were operating in the same neighborhoods. Money was poured into projects and programs that were ill-considered, lacked the support of local officials and authorities in Baghdad, and were poorly managed. The program to build capacity in national ministries, so critical to sustaining progress in Baghdad, was being run in complete isolation from the local reconstruction efforts. As the build phase floundered and sensing a vacuum in key reconstruction areas, the military began taking on reconstruction tasks for which it had no particular experience or expertise, in some cases making a bad situation worse.

An assessment of the state of reconstruction at the time in Baghdad and elsewhere in Iraq is contained in the Quarterly Report of the Special Inspector General for Iraq Reconstruction (SIGIR), dated January

2007.[1] Despite the massive energy being put into the build phase in Baghdad, the report noted only "limited progress" in several identified key areas, among them "ensuring the sustainability of reconstruction programs and projects," "building ministerial capacity," and "improving coordination of all U.S. agencies involved in reconstruction."[2] In support of these observations, SIGIR cited statistics showing that from August through December 2006 (the first 6 months of the Baghdad Security Plan), peak electrical power generation actually decreased by 20 percent. Power interruptions in Baghdad were common. At the end of 2006, on any given day, neighborhoods could expect only 8 hours of electricity. Crude oil production, so critical to funding the recovery of Baghdad and other major cities in Iraq, showed no measureable increase over the same time period, hovering at about one-half million barrels per day below established production targets which had been set at about 2.5 million barrels. Additionally, of the 126 health care facilities that had been promised to the Iraqi people, most of them in Baghdad, only seven had been opened by the end of 2006.[3]

What many senior officials and planners had hoped would become an upward spiral, as reconstruction in cleared areas won over local residents and contributed to more security, turned into the exact opposite. Disillusionment among the population who continued to suffer from horrendous living conditions, unemployment and ineffective local government and administration fueled unrest, instability, and thus the insurgency. In short, after the Ambassador and the Force Commander launched the Baghdad Security Plan as a new COIN campaign based on a sort of three legged stool—"Clear, Hold, Build"—the balance that needed to be struck between the legs to arrive at a successful campaign proved impossible to achieve. As a result, the violence in Baghdad continued to rage.

Reconstruction in one form or another has long been a part of war. When viewed, for example, as something that took place after conflict had subsided to mend the horrific wounds of a nation that had been ripped apart by civil war to make it whole again, or a rebuilding of one-time foes so that they could serve as part of the bulwark against an existential threat, reconstruction efforts have been viewed as among America's greatest triumphs. But reconstruction has also been reviled and repudiated as "nation-building" and blamed as the cause of "mission creep," held up by critics as an activity inconsistent with the American way of war.

Reconstruction has also gone by many names and played an integral role in a wide range of military operations. At the turn of the 20th century, during the Philippine Wars, reconstruction was the centerpiece of the "policy of attraction" and was balanced with the more familiar "policy of chastisement" to form the basis of the operational concept underlying America's first significant experience with an indigenous guerrilla and a recalcitrant population in an overseas military intervention. During the Vietnam War, the component of the Civil Operations and Revolutionary Development Support (CORDS) program known as "constructive activities" would be recognizable today as reconstruction. Peace enforcement, peace building, stabilization, pacification, and other types of operations whose purpose goes beyond just the defeat of an enemy army all involve reconstruction in one form or another. The new Army doctrine on operations includes discussion of "operational themes," one of which, peacetime military engagement, includes several types of operations that might include reconstruction as an integral component. But in no form of warfare has reconstruction been more important than in COIN. If successfully employed and accurately focused, reconstruction can take away an insurgent's cause and deny him what he seeks most fervently — the active and willing support of the population.

The recent publication of the latest U.S. Army doctrine on operations — *Field Manual (FM) 3-0, Operations; FM 3-07, Stability Operations;* and *FM 3-24 Counterinsurgency* (and its counterpart in *Joint Doctrine (JP) 3-24, Counterinsurgency*) — has solidified the importance of reconstruction to COIN. It is now seen as an integral part of this important form of warfare — an activity that when properly undertaken can win battles and wars, a determining factor on par with any of the elements of combat power or battlefield operating systems. Publication of these manuals is actually a case of Army doctrine catching up to the realties of a contemporary battlefield. For many years, small unit leaders have been practicing various reconstruction methods in both Operations ENDURING FREEDOM and IRAQI FREEDOM. However, success in achieving the desired effect on the fight has been uneven, and these attempts often have been frustrating efforts for these leaders. Too many times, reconstruction has proven an unwieldy, insufficient, or, in worse cases, a counterproductive effort, and it has been the subject of a fair amount of scrutiny and criticism at the tactical, operational and policy levels.

This monograph proposes to answer the following key questions about the role of reconstruction in counterinsurgency operations:

1. How has the role of reconstruction in U.S. COIN operations developed over the years?

2. How should the U.S. Army try to understand the role of reconstruction in COIN as we have come to know it in the 21st century?

3. Where does the Army fit into the larger reconstruction effort undertaken by other U.S. Government departments and agencies in modern COIN operations? Of the universe of key tasks associated with reconstruction in COIN, which should fall to the Army?

4. Does the Army have the necessary capabilities to accomplish the reconstruction tasks that it will be expected to accomplish in COIN?

5. What changes or refinements to U.S. Army doctrine, procedures, and organizations will make the Army a more effective partner in a reconstruction effort on a COIN battlefield?

Because of the many and varied demands for expertise and resources, reconstruction in COIN will of necessity be a multiagency and often international undertaking. It is impossible to adequately treat the role of reconstruction in COIN without at least addressing the issue of interagency cooperation, coordination, and roles and responsibilities. Chapter 4 is an attempt to address this matter without venturing into the well-trodden ground that has become the terrain of countless bureaucratic battles over who can or should be bearing what part of the burden of reconstruction. The bulk of this monograph will focus on the reconstruction challenges that the Army will most likely face during COIN — those tasks that should rightly fall to the Army as well as the ones that the Army will likely take on because they are critical to mission success but currently beyond the capability of civilian agencies to handle in a timely and effective manner.

Recent experiences in Iraq and Afghanistan have left many to doubt the worth of reconstruction, especially given the expense involved. To date, about $60 billion has been spent in Iraq and already about two-thirds of that amount in Afghanistan even though, at the time of this writing, the United States has yet to fully ramp up its efforts there.[4] Adding to this doubt is the concern that the military has assumed numerous responsibilities of civilian agencies when the latter have been unable to live up to expectations (these concerns were at times spurred on by complaints from the military itself), which entail the commitment of combat forces, resources and focus that would otherwise be dedicated to more traditional military tasks.

In this monograph, we treat reconstruction in COIN for what it currently is: a specific set of activities that have the intended effect of contributing to the achievement of critical objectives—securing the population and winning their support away from the insurgent; strengthening and extending the reach of legitimate foreign governments into areas where insurgent influence threatens; bolstering moderates and isolating extremists; and, perhaps most fundamentally, addressing the important sources of violence and conflict that have given the insurgent his primary cause. This being a fairly generally acceptable description of the role that reconstruction can play in COIN, looking for ways to get it right seems a worthwhile endeavor, especially in light of the publication of new doctrine and the recent experience gained by ground forces in Iraq and Afghanistan, too much of it through trial and error.

ENDNOTES - CHAPTER 1

1. *Special Inspector General for Iraq Reconstruction (SIGIR) Quarterly Report*, January, 2007. Statistics cited are from the summary entitled "Highlights," available from *www.sigir.mil/reports/ quarterlyreports/Jan07/pdf/Highlights_-_January_2007.pdf*.

2. *Ibid.*, p. 4.

3. *Ibid.*, p. 3.

4. *Ibid.*, According to the statistics cited on the home page, the U.S. Congress has appropriated $39 million of reconstruction to date.

CHAPTER 2

RECONSTRUCTION IN TIMES OF WAR:
A HISTORY

Throughout most of the history of warfare, the complete destruction of an enemy nation and army was often thought to be the best way to win a war and secure the peace. Reconstruction efforts as they are understood today are a natural outgrowth of an evolution in thinking about war and changed views about how best to gain stability, enhance national security, and build a peaceful order. The term has come to describe two very different concepts. The first is associated with actions that are undertaken at the end of hostilities, usually by the victor. More recently, reconstruction has been viewed as an integral part of certain types of military operations, to be executed during the course of hostilities usually as part of a larger military strategy. A brief, opening discussion of the history of reconstruction can shed light on some important understandings — and misunderstandings.

The Marshall Plan.

Reconstruction was a topic of conversation between the leaders of the Allied Powers — Roosevelt, Churchill, and Stalin — as they conducted their major summit meetings during the course of the war. Naturally the primary focus was the unconditional surrender of the Axis Powers, and the military means to achieve it. But even as the war raged, and before the landings at Normandy, the U.S. War Department had begun planning for the occupation of Germany. In 1943 Major General John H. Hildring became the first director of the new Civil Affairs division, charged by General Marshall with "planning the nonmilitary aspects of whatever occupations the Army would have to handle in the future."[1] There was considerable disagreement between key officials in the U.S. Government as to the underlying philosophy of the reconstruction of Europe, most of it being centered on the nature of the coming occupation of Germany. Leading War Department officials, remembering the results of the severe treatment of Germany after World War I and believing that harsh treatment set the conditions for the rise of Hitler and authoritarian rule in that and other European nations, were advocates for a restoration of civilian government and the revitalization of the German economy. An opposing view, famously championed by Secretary of the Treasury Henry Morgenthau, held that Germany had not been punished enough after World War I, and more severe measures should be implemented to "prevent Germany from starting World War III."[2] The two camps vied with each other, initially for Roosevelt's favor and then for that of Truman when he became President. But even by the time of the Potsdam Conference, the direction that reconstruction of Germany would take was unclear.[3]

It was only once the reconstruction started that the way ahead was clarified. Initially, the approach advocated by the Morgenthau camp seemed to be holding sway—the national institutions of the Nazi government were dismantled, Germany was divided into zones to be occupied by the victorious parties, and economic rebuilding was based upon the assumption that Germany's economy would be agrarian-based to ensure that the means to build another war machine would be denied. But as the occupation wore on and the suffering of the European populations became increasingly evident (none more so than in Germany) while the threat of Soviet expansionism loomed, the guiding philosophy of reconstruction changed. In 1947, *Joint Chiefs of Staff (JCS) Order 1779* was drafted which decreed that "an orderly and prosperous Europe requires the economic contributions of a stable and productive Germany."[4] The restrictions placed on production from German heavy industry were partly rescinded, and allowable steel production levels were increased significantly.[5] The provisions of the Marshall Plan, and the massive infusion of U.S. funds to support it, continued to hold sway until 1951 when the burdens of the Korean War running concurrently with expenditures dedicated to the reconstruction of Europe became too much for the American public to bear. Yet the overall effects of the Marshall Plan on the course of post-World War II history in Europe and beyond are well known. It was the single most important factor in the birth of a multinational economy that is one of the most vibrant in the world today. And it helped to usher in the political and economic consolidation and interdependence that have led to an unprecedented period of peace in a region of the world where most of the major battlegrounds of the most devastating wars in history are located.

Reconstruction in "Small Wars" — The U.S. Experience in the Philippines.

The American intervention in the Philippine Islands at the beginning of the 20th century does not figure particularly large in military history. Though it was truly a small war by many of the standards accepted by those who assign such classifications, the response of the U.S. Government and military to the insurrection that grew in the wake of Commodore George Dewey's victory over the Spanish fleet in Manila Bay in the spring of 1898 is significant well beyond the number of soldiers deployed or the attention it is paid by most military scholars.[6] Soldiers in the ranks of Army formations that were sent to fight with the Spanish occupiers, led by an officer corps whose most significant combat experience was gained in the U.S. Civil War, were about to become the first American counterinsurgent force in history.

Judging by the first contacts, the war seemed to be anything but unconventional. There were about 8,000 American Soldiers in Manila when the U.S. flag was raised over the city in August 1898 after a quick victory over Spanish forces there. By February, it had become clear that the Philippine rebels who had been battling the Spanish occupiers for many years prior to the U.S. intervention had a very different view of the future of their country than that of their American "liberators." On February 4, tensions that had been growing between U.S. forces inside the city and the Army of Liberation of the famous Philippine rebel leader Ernesto Aguinaldo erupted into full scale combat. Vastly outnumbering their opponents, Aguinaldo's forces had arrayed themselves in a loose ring completely surrounding the city. U.S. Major General Elwell S. Otis seized upon an opportunity to surprise his adversary by striking in mass first, ordering a frontal assault on the Liberation Army's defensive perimeter launched from outside Manila, and a simultaneous operation conducted by three regiments to secure the city itself. Both operations were supported by naval barrages and field artillery fire. Over the next week, the ensuing encounters, known collectively as the

Battle of Manila, consisted of repeated instances of U.S. forces offering conventional engagements and Agunaldo's Liberation Army accepting on exactly those terms. The resulting American victory in the field was completely predictable.[7]

But in Manila soon thereafter, a pattern started to emerge that in one form or another would challenge U.S. forces in the Philippines for the next half century. In response to the decisive defeats that his forces had suffered, Aguinaldo issued the order for all military aged men to join "the militia" while putting into place a guerrilla organization that would continue the fight against the American occupiers for years to come.[8] The ensuing guerrilla attacks were not long in coming. Four days after the end of the Battle of Manila, a captured document revealed to the U.S. commanders that the city's militias had been ordered to "rise and wage war without quarter" in the streets.[9] Meanwhile, in the neighboring Visayas Islands, a rural-based guerrilla movement in the "boondocks" was growing. The history of the ensuing insurgency that was carried out by this loose coalition is well-documented and has become known for its ferocity. It is well-known and understandable that the guerrilla fighters resorted to violent asymmetric methods. Also well known is that the response from U.S. forces, led first by Major General Otis and then famously by Major General Arthur McArthur, was severe. In fact, it is the tactics of the "howling wilderness," the introduction of water boarding as an interrogation technique, concentration camps, and the accepted (if not encouraged) technique of "civilizing 'em with the Krag" that are the most oft-recalled symbols of America's first encounter with COIN in the Philippines.[10]

Less well remembered is the experience of America's counterinsurgent army in Negros. A veteran of the Battle of Manila, Brigadier General James F. Smith was appointed the military governor of the SubDistrict of Negros on March 1, 1899. Garrisoned by only 400 troopers of the 1st California Infantry of that state's Volunteers, this smaller island of 320,000 inhabitants was rife with factional fighting and instability that was mainly the result of a combination of political rivalries between nationalist movements, attacks by guerrilla fighters, and criminal activity. Upon his arrival in Negros, Smith set out to establish on the island a showcase for American rule in the provinces.[11] He used American troops mostly to secure the population and key political and economic centers and rarely to conduct offensive operations. One of his first acts was to establish a 200-man local constabulary to take the lead in policing of the major towns. A local government was established, and measures taken to restore economic and commercial stability to the island. Smith fully embraced the notion of "benevolent assimilation"; his proud claim was that "all towns occupied by our troops and all the places where they have had an opportunity of fraternizing with the people have remained our steadfast friends." As military governor, he also dedicated considerable effort to what has become known as "capacity building" in local governments, the first objectives being eliminating corruption, trimming bloated bureaucracies, and a fair and effective system of taxation.[12]

In later years of the Philippine War, approaches like this one in Negros became the exception rather than the rule. Convinced that the insurgency had been beaten and that the effects of benevolent assimilation were winning over the population, General Otis requested relief from his duties claiming that "we no longer deal with organized insurrection."[13] In May 1900 General Arthur MacArthur took command in the Philippines and came to very different conclusions about the state of the insurgency and how to deal with it. Whether the increased violence and renewed insurgency that followed his assumption of command and continued until Aguinaldo's surrender in 1901 warranted the abandonment of much of the U.S. civic action campaign and the choice to resume large scale conventional operations or was a result of those decisions is open to question.[14] What is certain is that America had experienced its first COIN, and had at least learned that small wars could be as complex and challenging as large ones, and an approach to them deserved some serious thought.

A Brief History of the Writings about COIN and the Role of Reconstruction.

Early theorists of small wars paid scant attention to the topic of reconstruction. T. E. Lawrence was one of the few participants in early insurgencies who put his thinking on such warfare in writing. In recounting his participation in the Arab insurgency against the Ottoman Empire, he listed 27 articles that summarized what he had learned of insurgency while fighting with the Arabs during World War I. The list includes very detailed and personal advice about the nuances of fighting with Arab irregular forces, the most well-known being his caution, "Do not try to do too much with your own hands. Better the Arabs do it tolerably than that you do it perfectly."[15] It is interesting to note that this particular article has been cited often by current students and practitioners of COIN operations to support such notions as "putting an Iraqi (or Afghani) face" on reconstruction efforts. When taken in context, however, Lawrence was clearly providing advice about who should do most of the leading and fighting in battle. In fact, none of the 27 articles pays much attention at all to measures taken with the population in mind, much less reconstruction.[16]

It took another 50 years and the outbreak of the wars of national liberation that brought the decolonization of the Third World before a focus on the population as critical to insurgency and COIN, and the specific role of reconstruction, was introduced to the body of writings on COIN. The French military theorist David Galula has regularly been cited in current works on COIN with a frequency that surpasses the notice he received when he was writing in the 1960s. Drawing on experience gained in Algeria and writing for the RAND Corporation from his adopted home in the United States, Galula sought to present what he posited were the "rules of counterinsurgency warfare."[17]

In his foreword to Galula's text, one of today's preeminent experts on counterinsurgency, John Nagl, highlights the contribution that Galula made to military writings as being "his lucid instructions on how counterinsurgency forces can protect and hence gain the support of the populace, acquire information on the identity and location of insurgents, and thereby defeat the insurgency."[18] But Galula also emphasizes the utility to the counterinsurgent force of providing for the population beyond just security, touching on the value of providing for the needs and desires of the population—both the short-term ones (which he describes as providing "incentives") and those that are more enduring (effecting "reforms").

He describes these incentives and reforms as being designed to win "the wholehearted support of the population,"[19] and he recommends that they should begin as soon as practicable. Galula advises that "the counterinsurgent can at once start working on various projects in the economic, social, cultural, and medical fields, where results are not entirely dependent on the active cooperation from the population"[20] and specifically mentions easily organized activities, such as "cleaning the village or repairing the streets."[21]

But Galula makes a distinction between incentives that are offered to win the support of the population in the near term and the more enduring reform that is required to remove the causes of the insurgency. He uses Mao's formulation, the "unsolved contradiction," to characterize the causes, and observes that they may manifest themselves as one or more types of "problems" — social, political, racial, or economic.[22] He postulates that, "To deprive the insurgent of a good cause amounts to solving the country's basic problems."[23] But he is realistic about when such fundamental reform should be attempted, observing that attempts to effect reform in an unstable or unsecure environment will probably be ineffective, and maybe even counterproductive.

Finally, Galula offers observations about roles and missions in COIN, positing that "it is better to entrust civilian tasks to civilians," but also noting that, because the civilian bureaucracy is never up to "the personnel requirements of a counterinsurgency," that "to confine soldiers to purely military functions while urgent and vital tasks have to be done, and nobody else is available to undertake them, would be senseless." However, he warns against carrying this approach too far in duration or scope saying, ". . . to let the military direct the entire process . . . is so dangerous that it must be resisted at all costs."[24]

Reconstruction and the Vietnam War.

Galula died in 1967 when concerns were growing about the course of the war in Vietnam. Contrary to the earlier projections of General William Westmoreland, who had predicted victory by that year, it became increasingly clear that U.S. forces would need to play more than just a secondary role in the fighting going forward, which was becoming more than the Army of the Republic of Vietnam could handle. U.S. troop levels began to increase dramatically, and national leaders at the highest levels were looking for ways to stabilize the deteriorating situation in Vietnam.

Controlling the population became a matter of concern. The "strategic hamlets program" which had been initiated earlier in the 1960s was proving to be a failure. Similar to the program that had been carried out by the British in Malaya, the effort involved resettling rural populations from their small villages to nominally secure locations where the population could be isolated from the Viet Cong and more easily controlled. The program brought limited results because it was never properly resourced and proved wildly unpopular with the Vietnamese people who resented being uprooted. Strategic hamlets were rapidly infiltrated by insurgents who in many cases were welcomed by disgruntled inhabitants, and by 1963 the program was essentially dead.[25]

As troop levels increased, policymakers in Washington searched for programs that, in accordance with informed thinking on COIN warfare such as that found in the writings of Galula, could be effectively implemented to make inroads with the population, the sea in which the Viet Cong seemed to be swimming freely.

Enter Robert William Komer. Originally a staffer working directly for McGeorge Bundy in President Lyndon Johnson's National Security Council (NSC), Komer rose to prominence in Washington circles when he served temporarily as the National Security Advisor after Bundy's departure. While serving on the NSC, Komer focused primarily on how to coordinate and strengthen the effort of the civilian agencies in Washington in support of the growing military effort in Vietnam. He quickly became convinced that the solution to this coordination challenge could not be found in Washington but would have to be driven from inside the theater of war itself. In early 1967 he set to work on developing the mechanism to achieve this end, and left shortly thereafter to operationalize the concept in Vietnam himself.[26]

Military Assistance Command, Vietnam (MACV) Directive Number 10-12 was the order issued by General Westmoreland's headquarters that put into effect the organization and authorities that Komer felt were necessary to bring about pacification—the necessary condition for successful counterinsurgency in Vietnam. The stated purpose of MACV Directive 10-12 was "To provide for the integration of Civil Operations and Revolutionary Development Support (CORDS) activities within MACV."[27]

Though the acronym CORDS soon took on a life of its own, the original directive described an organization and assigned responsibilities that were designed to bring order to the civilian effort in Vietnam, which to that point had been relatively disorganized. Now commonly thought of as an integrated program in and of itself, the distinguishing characteristics of CORDS can be described as follows:

- The principle objective was rural "pacification," bringing security and stability to the country-side in order to deprive the Viet Cong of the support of the people.
- CORDS actually consisted of a series of programs, some of which were focused on reconstruction goals (for example, the "Takeoff Program," described below). Others focused on the security of the population (such as the founding of the paramilitary Regional and Popular Forces), and also included efforts to undermine and attack the Viet Cong military and political infrastructure (the *Chieu Hoi* and Phoenix programs).
- The reconstruction effort was regionally focused, and viewed as critical to the overall success of CORDS. Komer saw reconstruction (which he called the "constructive side" of CORDS) as "a series of interlocking programs . . . designed to generate both positive rural support of the GVN [Government of Vietnam] and antipathy towards the VC [Vietnamese Communists]."[28] So, *inter alia*, there was a carrot and stick effect desired: The idea was to win the loyalties of the local people away from the insurgents by offering them benefits and advantages that the Viet Cong could not, while gaining leverage through these efforts—that is, making the continuation of assistance conditional upon the continued cooperation of the population.[29]
- The organization that was created to implement CORDS was based on a fully integrated military and civilian architecture. The organization-

al diagram that was appended to MACV 10-12 depicted military and civilian officials working with and for each other at every level. The clearest signal of General Westmoreland's intention to make CORDS a civil-military operation was the position that he created for Komer himself — he served as one of two deputy force commanders with at least nominal command authority and the responsibility to give guidance and direction to military and civilian officials alike who were located lower in the chain.

The development and constructive side of CORDS was also notable for several characteristics which are of special interest to those familiar with reconstruction and its role in COIN today:

- Like the program overall, the reconstruction component was intended to be a civil-military effort. Teams composed of military officers and soldiers worked with Department of State and U.S. Agency for International Development (USAID) officials at the ground level, interfacing with Vietnamese district and village leaders on various development projects. Further, Komer felt strongly that the attempt made by some CORDS officials to divide up tasks between military and civilian activities in accordance with some strict formulation of their respective lanes would lead to "a whole series of mistakes."[30]
- Activities and programs that made up the reconstruction effort of CORDS were designed to meet the full range of reconstruction objectives — economic, infrastructure, governance, rule of law, and public information. These pro-

grams were primarily of two types. The first were those efforts that were focused on the longer-term changes and reforms that were needed to remove the sources of unrest and violence that made the insurgency possible in the first place — the types of actions that Galula saw as essential to remove the insurgent's cause. So, for example the Takeoff Program which was a key component of CORDS included as one of its eight platforms the achievement of Republic of Vietnam (RVN) policies and instrumentalities to carry out effective land reform. Another Takeoff project was to be the revitalization and repair of key road networks.[31] The second type of programs were those with more near-term, local, highly visible impacts that could win the hearts and minds of the local populace. An example program of this nature was the "Assistance in Kind" program which was notable for its smaller projects and emergency relief in villages across Vietnam. The Assistance in Kind program included provisions to give CORDS advisors "pocket money" that they could spend immediately on projects as they saw fit.[32]

- Though reconstruction and development were presumed to be most effectively and efficiently carried out in a secure environment, there was the realization that it would often be desirable, if not necessary, to begin building before an area was fully pacified. In a precursor to modern COIN doctrine, Komer's taxonomy of reconstruction activities included the formulation "clear, hold," but notably left out the third element of the modern day triad, "build." In Komer's discussion of CORDS, building was treated as an integral part of the "hold" activities that at times might also need to be carried out during the "clear" phase.[33]

- There were great pains taken to ensure that reconstruction activities were viewed as being led by legitimate officials of the Vietnamese government. The "RD" in CORDS, standing for "revolutionary development," may have struck Western observers as sounding somewhat unusual, but to the Vietnamese that choice of terminology was familiar and significant. On various occasions, Komer emphasized the point that the entire pacification effort was to be "a 100% Vietnamese show."[34]

In the end, CORDS was implemented with the goal of pacifying 10,000 hamlets and 2,000 villages in 250 districts and 44 provinces. At the program's height, the U.S. cadre consisted of 5,500 U.S. advisors working with a budget of $1.3 billion.[35] However, evaluating the overall effectiveness of the program is problematic. The measures of effectiveness used by officials of CORDS—embodied in the Hamlet Evaluation System—were hotly debated at the time and remain so to this day. What can be said, however, is that the general pacification effort in Vietnam—and CORDS specifically—fundamentally influenced the way strategists, theorists, and practitioners would think about COIN. As Robert Komer himself would say, "We didn't invent pacification, but we did put it on the map at long last on a major scale as an indispensable part of counterinsurgency strategy."[36]

The Legacy of Vietnam and "Nation Building."

The general aversion to the U.S. use of military force attributable to the outcome of the war in Vietnam has been well-documented and much discussed. The impact that Vietnam had on the thinking of some of the most influential policymakers of the 1980s and 1990s effectively constrained every president after Nixon at critical moments, especially when they wanted to keep the use of force on the table. Formal and informal guidelines like the Weinberger Doctrine (articulated in many places, but first by the Secretary of Defense in a speech to the national Press Club in 1984),[37] and General Colin Powell's oft-repeated thoughts on the use of military force, best articulated in an article he wrote for *Foreign Affairs* that appeared in the Winter 1992/93 edition, are examples of this effect. In general, these and similar prescriptions made a strong case that the use of military force should not be considered unless vital U.S. national security interests were at stake; other feasible options (political, diplomatic, or economic) had been exhausted; it could be presumed that the use of force was likely to be quick and overwhelming; and that the anticipated aftermath would involve no drawn out commitment of U.S. forces.

Yet the last quarter of the 20th century is notable not for the absence of occasions when the United States deployed forces to overseas contingencies, but for the numerous times that American soldiers were called on to undertake "small wars" of the type that took them far away from home and from the practiced core competencies in major combat operations that they had developed during the Cold War. Grenada, Panama, Somalia, Haiti, Bosnia, and Kosovo are only the most well known examples that can be cited. There were also numerous operations where the presence of U.S. forces was less commonly known or openly acknowledged. Army units, especially the Special Forces, conducted operations as part of a program known at the time as internal defense and development (IDAD). IDAD involved the employment of U.S. forces to support a host nation's efforts to identify the root causes of unrest and violence to take away the cause of an insurgent group, ideally before a full blown insurgency could take root. One of the most successful examples of the effectiveness of IDAD is the case of U.S. 1980s operations conducted in El Salvador.[38]

But in the eyes of the American people and reflected in the military and political policy positions that their leaders took, the very real casualties of the Vietnam War were those activities whose purpose had even a slight scent of attempts to "win hearts and minds" or activities that smacked of "nation building." Especially egregious in the eyes of politicians, military leaders, and, to a large degree, the general public alike, were those activities that might threaten to entangle the military in some sort of "quagmire" of political or developmental issues, matters that drew soldiers into activities that were outside of warfighting, or efforts to effect improvements that could be seen as the responsibility of the government or the people of the nation that our forces had invaded. What is now known as reconstruction fell well outside the boundaries of any comfort zone so delineated.

It is true that there was some appetite for nation building under the type of very strictly limited, almost *sui generis*, conditions that existed in the aftermath of the war to liberate Kuwait in 1990-91. The rebuilding of Kuwait was perhaps the most successful reconstruction effort undertaken since the Marshall Plan.[39] Kuwait Task Force teams were set up to conduct the full range of reconstruction activities – public security and safety, human services, infrastructure, public services, and commerce.[40] But there was no fighting to speak of while the reconstruction went on; certainly there was no insurgency to contend with. In terms of development, Kuwait started the war as one of the most advanced nations in the Middle East, and much of the infrastructure that had existed before the war, though heavily damaged, could be repaired or refurbished as opposed to requiring replacement. Private firms and companies willing to do the work in Kuwait were plentiful. Outside of the U.S. Army Corps of Engineers and some Civil Affairs units, very few soldiers were involved in the post-war mission. The Kuwaitis proved willing and able hosts, and had access to sufficient funding so that sharing the burdens of reconstruction never became an issue in the United States. Perhaps most importantly, the bulk of the reconstruction effort was over within less than a year after the end of hostilities in Kuwait and Iraq.

The example of operations in Haiti is far more illustrative – and typical – of the post-Vietnam attitude of military and civilian officials to reconstruction as a supporting effort to military operations, or as a longer-term effort to address the root sources of instability undertaken by a civil-military team. On September 18, 1994, after repeated unheeded warnings to the leadership of Haiti's junta to yield governance of that nation to the democratically elected president, Secretary of Defense Perry signed an executive order launching a forced entry operation which was intended to end the military dictatorship. In the event, no forced entry was required (a last minute deal led to the departure of the junta); nonetheless, U.S. forces were still deployed to Haiti into what was classified as a "less-than-permissive threat environment."[41] Based on these conditions, and following several violent incidents involving U.S. Soldiers that called for the use of deadly force, the commander of U.S. forces, Lieutenant General Hugh Shelton, announced that force protection would be his top priority. The small number of nascent reconstruction activities that were ongoing virtually died. The occupying forces were to engage in no activities that could be construed as nation-building. For a time the vast majority of regular U.S. Army Soldiers who had deployed to Haiti were even instructed not to leave their bases. U.S. military forces were not involved in policing or in the training of police. Based on their assertion that restoring electricity and providing drinking water to the population of Port-au-Prince was a civilian task, the military command in Haiti had to be ordered by higher headquarters to undertake the mission when it became clear that civilian agencies would be delayed in their arrival.[42] The perceived inability or unwillingness of U.S. forces to attend to the basic needs of the Haitian people led to a deterioration of support from the local population that may well have had a severe negative impact had the occupation lasted more than the few months that it did. Though many analysts have judged operations in Haiti a military success, it was clear then—and perhaps clearer today—that the failure to address any of the more fundamental problems existing in Haiti at that time has contributed to a level of instability that continues to plague that small island nation to this day.

The Impact of September 11, 2001.

Many of the nagging concerns about small wars and the role that nation building-like activities could play in them have been put aside, at least temporarily, in the aftermath of the attacks of September 11, 2001 (9/11). There was an almost immediate understanding that the United States was entering a period when addressing instability in troubled parts of the world could be construed as being critical to national security interests, especially when that instability might give rise to or provide safe harbor for extremist fighters advocating radical ideologies. For the most part with eyes open, senior political decisionmakers launched efforts on all fronts to craft policies that were intended to put the nation and all branches of its government on a path to bring stability to regions deemed critical to the United States. And military leaders responded with directives and doctrine to support that approach. At the center of this policy and doctrine is a firm endorsement of the important role of reconstruction.

The two documents that can best be said to have captured the essentials of this direction are *National Security Presidential Directive 44* (NSPD-44) and *DoD Directive 3000.05* (DoDD 3000.05), both of which were issued in late 2005. NSPD-44 puts it plainly. The first sentence in the statement of policy reads: "The United States has a significant stake in enhancing the capacity to assist in stabilizing and reconstructing countries or regions, especially those at risk of, in, or in transition from conflict or civil strife, and to help them establish a sustainable path toward peaceful societies, democracies, and market economies"[43] This clear endorsement of reconstruction is followed by specific guidance on roles and responsibilities of the various departments of the U.S. Government to support those activities. The Department of State is given the responsibility to coordinate and lead what the document calls "stability and reconstruction operations." The relationship between State and the Department of Defense (DoD) is described as follows: "The Secretaries of State and Defense will integrate stabilization and reconstruction contingency plans with military contingency plans when relevant and appropriate. The Secretaries of State and Defense will develop a general framework for fully coordinating stabilization and reconstruction activities and military operations at all levels where appropriate."[44]

Fully consistent with the guidance in NSPD-44, DoDD 3000.05 states that, "Stability operations are a core military mission that the Department of Defense shall be prepared to conduct and support."[45] The document goes on to list the activities that are considered to be components of stability operations (establishing good governance and rule of law, repairing infrastructure, economic revitalization, and other reconstruction activities feature prominently among these), and, though emphasizing the primarily civilian nature of these tasks and stipulating the comparative advantage resident in civilian departments to accomplish them, it nevertheless states that, "US military forces shall be prepared to perform all tasks necessary to establish or maintain order when civilians cannot do so."[46]

This guidance was issued at about the time when violent attacks in Iraq against coalition forces and the Iraqi people, carried out by Sunni rejectionists and Shia radicals, were increasing, and as it was becoming increasingly clear that operations in Afghanistan were amounting to something more than just mopping up the residue of the deposed Taliban dictatorship. U.S.

decisionmakers, especially within the military, were becoming increasingly aware that they were engaging in two COIN wars simultaneously, and key political leaders fully expected that the military would be prepared to at least play a strong supporting role in bringing about a stable environment in these two regions, if not take the leading role in both efforts.

Insofar as was possible at the time, the military establishment initiated several programs designed to adapt the force to the demands of the political leadership. Reshaping a military that at the start of the 21st century had remained essentially unchanged since the victory in Operation DESERT STORM has proved difficult, and understandably has progressed in fits and starts. It takes time to modify organizations, restructure training programs, develop leaders, arm and equip soldiers with the type of kit that is suited to the special rigors of COINs, and then make the appropriate budget adjustments. Progress has been uneven across the lines of effort that have been traditionally used by defense (and especially Army) planners to define new requirements—the so called DOTML-PF.[47] The theory of COIN warfare found in treatises like those of David Galula, and the lessons learned about pacification, development, and reconstruction in Vietnam, have been resurrected from relative obscurity and become the passion of both civilian and military experts. Perhaps the most notable outcome of this rediscovered interest is the series of doctrinal manuals that have been recently published that today serve to guide the current operations of the military, especially ground forces, despite the fact that transformation to meet the requirements of the operations described in these manuals is lagging. The doctrine, which has become in effect the leading edge of a fundamental transformation of U.S. Armed Forces, has much to say about the role of reconstruction in successful operations designed to defeat insurgencies and establish stability. Chapter 3 will examine this doctrine in some detail.

ENDNOTES - CHAPTER 2

1. James Dobbins, Michael A. Poole, Austin Long, and Benjamin Runkle, *After the War*, Santa Monica, CA: The RAND Corporation, 2008, pp. 17-18.

2. *Ibid.*, p. 20.

3. *Ibid.*, p. 26.

4. This extracted quote from *JCS Order 1779* is taken from the *Wikipedia* entry entitled "The Marshall Plan," available from *en.wikipedia.org/wiki/Marshall_Plan*.

5. Ray Salvatore Jennings, *The Road Ahead: Lessons in Nation Building from Japan, Germany, and Afghanistan for Post-War Iraq, Peaceworks No. 49*, Washington, DC: United States Institute of Peace, 2003, p. 15.

6. Brian McAllister Linn, *The Philippine War, 1899-1902*, Lawrence: University of Kansas Press, 2000. This work is generally considered to be the authoritative history on the early U.S. experience in the Philippines.

7. *Ibid.* The Battle of Manila is described on p. 42 ff.

8. *Ibid.*, p. 58.

9. *Ibid.*, pp. 72-73.

10. *Ibid.*, p. 322. The Krag (Krag-Jorgenson) is the name of a bolt action rifle that was in use by American forces in the Philippines at the time.

11. *Ibid.*, p. 82-83.

12. *Ibid.*, p. 82.

13. *Ibid.*, p. 206.

14. *Ibid.*, pp. 213-215.

15. A copy of T. E. Lawrence's, "The 27 Articles," is available from *wwi.lib.byu.edu/index.php/The_27_Articles_of_T.E._Lawrence.*

16. *Ibid.*

17. David Galula, *Counterinsurgency Warfare Theory and Practice*, Westport, CT: Praeger Security International, 1964 and 2006, p. xiii.

18. *Ibid.*, p. vii.

19. *Ibid.*, p. 61.

20. *Ibid.*, p. 84.

21. *Ibid.*, p. 2.

22. *Ibid.*, p. 14.

23. *Ibid.*, p. 46.

24. *Ibid.*, p. 62.

25. This observation comes from Robert Komer in *Organization and Management of the "New Model" Pacification Program*, Washington, DC: The RAND Corporation, 1970, p. 13, cited extensively below.

26. *Ibid.*, p. 50-51.

27. *MACV Directive 10-12*, available from *www.mtholyoke.edu/acad/intrel/pentagon2/pent12.htm.*

28. Komer, p. 168.

29. *Ibid.* Chapter 9 discusses leverage.

30. *Ibid.*, p. 20.

31. *Ibid.*, p. 80.

32. *Ibid.*, p. 148.

33. *Ibid.*, p. 63.

34. *Ibid.*, p.115.

35. *Ibid.*, p. 220.

36. *Ibid.*, p. 246.

37. The Weinberger speech is available from *www.pbs.org/ wgbh/pages/frontline/shows/military/force/weinberger.html.*

38. Janet A. McDonnell, *After Desert Storm: The US Army and the Reconstruction of Kuwait,* is the most authoritative treatment of this topic, Washington, DC: Department of the Army Publication, U.S. Government Printing Office, 1999.

39. McDonnell, p. 38.

40. Dobbins *et al.*, p. 58.

41. *Ibid.*, p. 59.

42. NSPD 44 is available from *www.fas.org/irp/offdocs/nspd/ nspd-44.html.*

43. *Department of Defense Directive (DoDD) 3000.05, Military Support for Stability, Security, Transitions, and Reconstruction,* Washington, DC: Department of Defense, November 28, 2005.

44. *National Security Presidential Directive/NSPD-44,* para. entitled, "Coordination between the Secretary of State and the Secretary of Defense," December 7, 2005, available from *www.fas.org/ irp/offdocs/nspd/nspd-44.html.*

45. DoDD 3000.05.

46. DoDD 3000.05, para. 4.3, November 28, 2005, available from *fhp.osd.mil/intlhealth/pdfs/DoDD3000.05.pdf*. This DoDD was superseded by an update in September 2009 that omits the specific language of the earlier document but preserves the expansive scope of the guidance. See, for example, para. 4.a (3) which states that the military will be prepared to "lead stability operations activities to establish civil security and civil control, restore essential services, repair and protect critical infrastructure, and deliver humanitarian assistance until such time as it is feasible to transition lead responsibility to other U.S. Government agencies, foreign governments and security forces, or international governmental organizations."

47. DOTLM-PF is a U.S. Army acronym; it stands for doctrine, organizations, training, leader development, materiel, personnel, and facilities.

CHAPTER 3

A DOCTRINAL REVIEW

The recent publication of new U.S. Army and Marine Corps doctrine has been a significant contribution to the Army's understanding of modern warfare as we are experiencing it now and are likely to know it for some time to come. The new doctrine in *Field Manual (FM) 3-0, Operations*; *FM 3-07, Stability Operations*; and *FM 3-24, Counterinsurgency*, provides a coherent description of the relationship between different types of operations within the context of how ground forces will operate as part of joint, combined, and interagency teams along the full spectrum of conflict. Army doctrine has heavily influenced new Joint manuals that have followed; for example, *Joint Publication (JP) 3-24, Counterinsurgency* adopts the concepts developed by the Army and Marine Corps almost wholesale. The doctrine has also been carefully written to ensure that Army concepts are aligned with the latest thinking in the interagency community on civil-military operations. This chapter presents an assessment of the treatment of reconstruction in this new doctrine, and the degree to which the new doctrine advances an understanding of the role that it plays in counterinsurgency (COIN).

THE ARMY OPERATIONAL CONCEPT

FM 3-0 discusses the "spectrum of conflict" and identifies "operational themes" along the spectrum. Figure 3.1 shows the graphic depiction of that relationship.

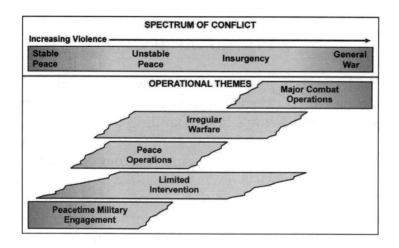

Figure 3.1. The Spectrum of Conflict and Operational Themes. [1]

Later in FM 3-0 the Army's operational concept is introduced as "full spectrum operations," which is described as consisting of three components—offensive, defensive, and stability operations—when it is executed in what the FM calls "joint campaigns (overseas)." (As it pertains to homeland security within the United States, the components become offense, defense, and civil support.) The operational environment and nature of the type of conflict at hand determines the specific relationship between the components in any given operation. (See Figure 3.2.)

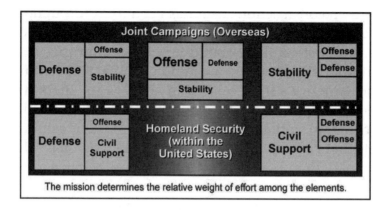

**Figure 3.2. Full Spectrum Operations —
the Army's Operational Concept.**[2]

FM 3-0 is remarkable for the clarity and simplicity of its explanation of the relationship between the three components of full spectrum operations, and the unprecedented importance that is placed on the role of stability operations. Unlike previous versions of the Army's capstone manual on operations, the new version of FM 3-0 goes into some detail in describing stability operations, placing them on the same plane as offensive and defensive operations in terms of their importance to the Army's operational concept. Later in FM 3-0, the five primary stability tasks are introduced: civil security, civil control, restore essential services, support to governance, and support to economic and infrastructure development.

RECONSTRUCTION AND FULL SPECTRUM OPERATIONS

The first important contribution of the new doctrine to an understanding of reconstruction is the most basic—a definition. As discussed in Chapter 2, the term "reconstruction" as it has been used throughout the majority of U.S. military history, has been applied to the post-conflict rebuilding of a vanquished foe. Additionally, since the beginning of the 20th century and America's involvement in small wars, there has been frequent mention made in doctrine and other writing on military matters of the important salutary role that various nonmilitary or "nonkinetic" activities can play in military operations, especially in irregular warfare. In these writings, these so-called nonkinetic activities are frequently referenced and largely understood to fall under the heading "reconstruction," but are never specifically classified as such. As a result, until the publication of FMs 3-0, 3-07, and 3-24, the use of the term "reconstruction" often engendered confusion. An example is the understanding of what provincial reconstruction teams (PRTs) are and what they do in Iraq and Afghanistan. The uninitiated often think of them as focused on rebuilding things, when in fact these small, multipurpose interagency teams have a much broader focus.[3]

FM 3-07 goes a long way to clearing up the conceptual confusion by providing the first doctrinal definition of reconstruction, found in the glossary of that manual:

> The process of rebuilding degraded, damaged, or destroyed political, socioeconomic, and physical infrastructure of a country or territory to create the foundation for long-term development.[4]

There are two significant points to note about this definition, and one key implication. The first point is that the FM 3-07 language makes no association between reconstruction and any particular phase of warfare, reinforcing the Army's conceptualization that it is not just a post-conflict or post-crisis activity. The second point is that the definition captures a broad range of activities, focused on addressing the needs of a population and building capacity in the institutions of their society. This places the concept of reconstruction well beyond the notion of simply the physical rebuilding of structures—houses, roads, factories, and the like. The implication is that the new doctrine places reconstruction at the center of the Army's operational concept, on par with any of the most fundamental activities that contribute to full spectrum operations. A comparison between the discussion of reconstruction in FM 3-07 and the description of stability operations in that document and in FM 3-0 underscores this point: The component activities listed in the doctrinal definition of reconstruction are exactly the same as three of the five categories of tasks of stability operations.

FULL SPECTRUM OPERATIONS, COIN, AND RECONSTRUCTION

Counterinsurgency is described in FM 3-0 as a type of operation falling into the category of "irregular warfare," one of the five operational themes. The attempt made in FM 3.0 to establish connections between points along the spectrum of conflict (unstable peace, general war," etc.) and operational themes (e.g., irregular war, peace operations, and major combat operations) engenders some conceptual confusion for those who are thinking about COIN and the role that reconstruction plays in it. For example, it is certainly possible to envision COIN as playing a major role in a peace enforcement operation (a different operational theme) being carried out in an environment described as "unstable peace" on the spectrum of conflict. Nonetheless, it still follows that, like other full spectrum operations, the conduct of COIN will always involve different mixes of offense, defense, and stability tasks depending on the mission and the nature of the operational environment.

COIN is described only briefly in either FM 3-0 or FM 3-07, most likely in deference to the treatment it gets in the much lauded FM 3-24, a manual which perhaps more than any other in the history of Army doctrine has virtually taken on a life of its own. Something between doctrine and a philosophy of war, FM 3-24 has much to say about the elements of reconstruction, while barely using the term itself at all—not even once in the doctrinal sense introduced in FM 3-07.

The rationale for conducting reconstruction in COIN is stated repeatedly, but its essence boils down to three reasons: First, because it is the right thing to do. Paragraph 2-41 notes that "Human decency and the laws of war require land forces to assist the populace in their AO's [areas of operation]. . . . to address human needs." The second reason cited is that reconstruction persuades the population to support the counterinsurgent and reject the guerilla:

> COIN is fought among the populace. Counterinsurgents take upon themselves responsibility for the people's well-being in all its manifestations. These include the following:
> - Security from insurgent intimidation and coercion, as well as from nonpolitical violence and crime.
> - Provision for basic economic needs.
> - Provision of essential services, such as water, electricity, sanitation, and medical care.
> - Sustainment of key social and cultural institutions.

- Other aspects that contribute to a society's basic quality of life.[5]

The third reason or purpose offered is that, as it is defined in FM 3-07, reconstruction can address the fundamental sources of violence and unrest in the nation, thereby removing the insurgent's cause:

> While security is essential to setting the stage for overall progress, lasting victory comes from a vibrant economy, political participation, and restored hope. . . . Soldiers and Marines should prepare to execute many nonmilitary missions to support COIN efforts. Everyone has a role in nation building, not just Department of State and civil affairs personnel.[6]

Elsewhere in FM 3-24, there is discussion of the nature of the role that the specific elements of reconstruction play in the overall COIN effort. As to be expected, the COIN "lines of operations" track closely with the elements of full spectrum operations, and the lines associated with reconstruction are a virtual one for one match (essential services, governance, and economic development in FM 3-24 and "restore essential services," "support to governance," and "support to economic and infrastructure development" in FM 3-0). But perhaps the most memorable endorsement for the importance of reconstruction in COIN comes in the section of FM 3-24 entitled "Paradoxes of Counterinsurgency" where the authors note: "Some of the best weapons for counterinsurgents do not shoot."[7]

WHERE THE DOCTRINE IS STRONG.

The strength of the Army's doctrine as it is presented in FMs 3-0, 3-07, and 3-24 is in the clear description of a new operational environment and the comprehensive view conveyed of how the Army will operate within that environment. All three of these works have risen to the level of "capstone manuals" and, as such, serve the purposes to which such doctrine has been traditionally intended. As has been the case in the past, most of the "how to" discussions are left for other venues—supporting doctrine, schools, and unit training being the most important of these.

As regards reconstruction, the salient points that emerge from the description of reconstruction in the new doctrine are:

1. As a collection of activities now grouped under a doctrinal heading, reconstruction plays a vital role in Army operations and must be synchronized with other military actions to achieve the commander's overall COIN objectives. Specifically, skillfully conducted reconstruction can be an important part of operations conducted in an environment of "stable peace" (for example, as an integral part of a security assistance program) as well as a supporting effort to counterinsurgency operations conducted during periods of limited intervention or irregular warfare, where reconstruction activities can be designed to defeat an insurgent by winning over a population that might other wise be indifferent—or even hostile—to the cause of the counterinsurgent, thereby isolating the insurgent from what he needs most: the support of the populace. That is, a critical purpose of reconstruction in COIN is "to win the hearts and minds" of the people.

2. Reconstruction is also the most direct approach to the root causes of an insurgency or the instability that spawns it. Successful reconstruction can remove the basic causes that the insurgent espouses, thereby marginalizing him, and can add to the legitimacy and support of the local and national instruments of the government, thereby furthering progress towards the counterinsurgent's campaign objectives. To that end, strengthening national institutions and building capacity in legitimate government — sometimes called "nation building" — is a second legitimate purpose of reconstruction in COIN.

3. A secure environment supports effective reconstruction, but reconstruction must also be thought of as a sort of combat multiplier that is used by counterinsurgent forces to *establish* security. This means that reconstruction will often take place as *part of* combat operations.

4. To defeat the insurgency, the counterinsurgent must reach the point where combat and security operations are the supporting effort; reconstruction to address the fundamental sources of conflict underlying the insurgency is the supported effort. But en route to that point, at times reconstruction must be undertaken as a supporting effort to combat operations, necessitating what has been called "reconstruction under fire."[8]

5. It follows, then, that reconstruction activities, projects, and programs need to be planned with two effects in mind — the impact on longer term objectives that are related to the causes of the insurgency, and the more immediate impact that can be had through reconstruction in support of combat and security operations in the near term. Decisions about reconstruction activities made by tactical commanders designed to achieve near-term effects on the populace must be

informed by an understanding of the implications for reconstruction efforts that are designed to achieve the longer term effect of eliminating the sources of violence and instability, and vice versa.

LOOMING ISSUES FOR THE PRACTITIONER

As it treats reconstruction, the new doctrine reveals some issues that have made it difficult for those who must deal in the world of the how to — how they must execute and prepare themselves and their formations to implement reconstruction if they are to achieve success in COIN.

The first issue has to do with the sheer number of tasks that reconstruction in COIN involves. Reconstruction tasks that are specified in the doctrine more than double the total number of tasks that tactical units must be prepared to perform in order to conduct stability operations. (It is worthy of note that, according to the new FM 3-0, tasks associated with stability and civil security operations outnumber those that are associated with offensive and defensive operations.)

The second issue that the new doctrine raises is the complexity of the tasks that collectively comprise reconstruction in COIN. Implied in the manuals is the notion that tactical units which are undertaking COIN operations must be prepared to execute a wide range of reconstruction tasks, varying in levels of sophistication and degree of required expertise from organizing and conducting trash collection to establishing work programs to support agricultural development in the host nation, or supporting public sector investment programs. This range of reconstruction tasks raises serious questions about the ability to ready any tactical unit — in terms of manning, training, organizing and equipping — to undertake certain of the reconstruction tasks that are called for by the latest doctrine.

Third, the matter of who has primary responsibility for different reconstruction tasks — and what exactly that should signify to military commanders preparing for COIN — is discussed extensively in FMs 3-07 and 3-24. In FM 3-07, reconstruction tasks are classified as one of three types:

1. Tasks for which military forces retain primary responsibility.

2. Tasks for which civilian agencies or organizations likely retain responsibility, but military forces are prepared to execute.

3. Tasks for which civilian agencies or organizations retain primary responsibility.[9]

FM 3-24 sends the same message about responsibilities for reconstruction tasks, stating in Chapter 1:

> The purpose of America's ground forces is to fight and win the Nation's wars. Throughout history, however, the Army and Marine Corps have been called on to perform many tasks beyond pure combat; this has been particularly true during the conduct of COIN operations. COIN requires Soldiers and Marines to be ready both to fight and to build — depending on the security situation and a variety of other factors.[10]

and later in Chapter 2:

> Political, social, and economic programs are most commonly and appropriately associated with civilian organizations and expertise; however, effective implementation of these programs is more important than who performs the tasks. If adequate civilian capacity is not available, military forces fill the gap. COIN programs for political, social, and economic well-being are essential to developing the local capacity that commands popular support when accurately perceived.[11]

The most revealing indication of what will be in store for military commanders by way of reconstruction in COIN is the conclusion about responsibilities drawn from FM 3-24 which sums up the preferred division of labor as: "Whenever possible, civilian agencies or individuals with the greatest applicable expertise should perform a task," but follows this statement closely with a discussion of the "realistic division of labor." This notion is introduced with an admonition: "The preferred or ideal division of labor is frequently unattainable," and includes advice to commanders to prepare to accomplish critical reconstruction tasks themselves. This mission to be prepared to take on so-called "civilian tasks" is accompanied by a quote attributed to David Galula, "The soldier must then be prepared to become . . . a social worker, a civil engineer, a schoolteacher, a nurse, a boy scout."[12]

The discussion in the manuals of the division of labor in reconstruction in COIN is problematic on three levels. First, it places the tactical commander in a real quandary about how to prepare for accomplishing reconstruction tasks in a COIN environment. Whipsawed back and forth between the counsel to be prepared to do everything but deferring to civilians whenever possible, a commander might well be excused for being inclined to err on the side of more preparation, and that is what most will do — until they take full measure of the universe of tasks for which they must prepare, which is offered in the doctrine without any particularly useful guidelines about how to establish the relative priority of these tasks. The second problem is the understandable conclusion that a young leader might draw from a reading of the doctrine that most of the tasks that should be left to civilian organizations and agencies will end up devolving on tactical unit commanders. The suggestion to commanders is that civilian agencies will usually not be able to hold up their end of the mission, and therefore soldiers will have to be prepared to pick up the slack. A full understanding of the relative capabilities, missions, and competencies of civilian agencies involved in reconstruction with respect to their military partners usually can put this observation in perspective. But experienced practitioners who are willing to be honest about attitudes that are derived from this perception are well aware of the corrosive effects that are associated with it. Finally, and related to the first two problems, military commanders who have prepared the best that they can for complex reconstruction tasks in COIN and who encounter a vacuum on the battlefield somewhere within the reconstruction effort, having been encouraged by their reading of current doctrine, are apt to jump into the breach. At times this may be the necessary and the right thing to do. But inherent in this approach is also the significant risk of doing more harm than would be done if no action were taken at all, especially in complex situations requiring experience and expertise that is not normally resident in tactical units.

Fourth, it follows from this discussion of responsibilities in the doctrine that there will be issues that will emerge related to "who's in charge?" of the overall reconstruction effort being conducted in support of COIN. Here, an attempt made in FM 3-07 to shed some light on a related matter actually highlights the problems that will inevitably occur and the need for dedicated and agreed upon mechanisms to manage reconstruction in COIN. The manual states that:

Reconstruction is the process of rebuilding degraded, damaged, or destroyed political, socioeconomic, and physical infrastructure of a country or territory to create the foundation for long-term development.

Stabilization is the process by which underlying tensions that might lead to resurgence in violence and a breakdown in law and order are managed and reduced, while efforts are made to support preconditions for successful long-term development.

Together, reconstruction and stabilization comprise the broad range of activities defined by the Department of Defense as stability operations.[13]

Introduction of the term "reconstruction and stabilization" is part of a well-intentioned attempt made in FM 3-07 to make some connection between work that is now being done in the civilian community and the closely related established military doctrine on stability operations and COIN.[14] But, besides raising the issue of how the reader of FM 3-07 is to make any meaningful distinction between these two processes based on the description of reconstruction and stabilization provided in this paragraph (which risks doing some damage to the later attempt in the manual to clearly define reconstruction), the discussion will no doubt be perplexing to the military readers in that the exact form and substance of a type of operation that is critical to successful COIN (that is, stability operations, which have recently been elevated to "a core U.S. military mission" in DoDD 3000.05) will be determined by the Secretary of State, who has been designated by the President in NSPD-44 as having the responsibility "to coordinate and strengthen efforts of the United States Government to prepare, plan for, and conduct reconstruction and stabilization assistance and related activities."[15]

Finally, a survey of the existing doctrine leaves the reader feeling a real need for more on how to integrate the reconstruction effort with other military actions being taken in COIN in order to achieve maximum effect on the populace and the insurgent. The number and complexity of tasks, multiple agencies and organizations that are involved, confusing lines of responsibility, and the issues raised about who will manage reconstruction on the battlefield does not bode well for a coordinated, coherent effort that can be integrated with combat operations to meet the objectives of a COIN campaign. It would be easy to understand why, after a reading of existing doctrine on reconstruction in COIN, a reader might be left looking for something beyond the theoretical and philosophical—a framework of sorts that helps him better understand the nature of reconstruction in COIN and how it works.

In the 1980s and 1990s when doctrine writers were facing a similar complex conceptual challenge to understand and explain the integration of multiple actions on the battlefield, they developed the "battlefield operating systems" (BOS), each of which was described in terms of a "concept" (for example, a concept of fires or concept of support) that has proven extraordinarily useful and familiar to all practitioners of combined arms operations to this day. To understand and explain how to coordinate and synchronize the reconstruction effort with combat and security operations in COIN—where the need for integration is, if anything, even more critical—some parallel construct to the BOS, or a concept of reconstruction, could be useful.

As is usually the case, the practitioners of COIN—military and civilian—are generally not waiting for more doctrine or additional guidance to help them deal with these conceptual issues. They are, for the most part, moving out and finding innovative and creative ways to deal with them. But these approaches are ad hoc and therefore only imperfectly captured and shared with others who are facing the same challenges. Additionally, without some sort of recognized Army concept of reconstruction it is difficult to make some of the key manning, equipping, and training decisions that are necessary to assist commanders to use this valuable tool on the COIN battlefield. So the development of an Army concept of reconstruction, within the context of the larger reconstruction effort that must take place in successful COIN, might not only enhance the effectiveness of tactical units in battle but would also assist the Army's leadership to make better choices about how to set these units up for success in their efforts.

No single analyst or doctrine writer could outline the parameters of a construct of reconstruction better than a group of practitioners called together to tackle a tough set of problems in a COIN environment. As part of the process of writing this monograph, the author included an attempt to make use of just such a resource. The results are described in the next chapter.

ENDNOTES - CHAPTER 3

1. *Field Manual (FM) 3-0, Operations*, Washington, DC: Department of the Army, 2008, Figure 2-2.

2. *Ibid.*, Figure 3-1.

3. For an illustrative discussion of this type of confusion, see the SIGIR Audit of PRT's published on October 29, 2006, p. 1, available from *www.sigir.mil/reports/pdf/audits/06-034.pdf*.

4. *Field Manual (FM) 3-07, Stability Operations*, Washington, DC: HQ Department of the Army, Glossary, October 2008, p. Glossary-9.

5. *Field Manual (FM) 3-24/Marine Corps Warfighting Publication (MCWP) 3-33.5, Counterinsurgency*, Washington, DC: Department of the Army, para. 2-6.

6. *Ibid.*, para. 3-72.

7. *Ibid.*, para. 1-153.

8. David C. Gompert, Terrence K. Kelly, Brooke Stearns Lawson, Michelle Parker, Kimberly Colloton, *Reconstruction Under Fire: Unifying Civil and Military Counterinsurgency*, Santa Monica, CA: The RAND Corporation, 2009.

9. FM 3-07, para 3-8.

10. FM 3-24, para 1-105.

11. FM 3-24, para 2-5.

12. FM 3-24, para 2-41.

13. FM 3-07, para 1-56.

14. The term "reconstruction and stabilization" is not an Army doctrinal term per se. The term is found in multiple interagency documents and is most often used by the Army only in discussions of interagency or civilian agency activities.

15. *National Security Presidential Directive-44: Management of Interagency Efforts Concerning Reconstruction and Stabilization*, Washington, DC: The White House, December 7, 2005, unnumbered para. describing the responsibilities of the Secretary of State, available from *www.fas.org/irp/offdocs/nspd/nspd-44.html*.

CHAPTER 4

CONDUCTING RECONSTRUCTION IN COUNTERINSURGENCY — AN EXERCISE

In an attempt to gain a greater understanding of the conduct of reconstruction operations in counterinsurgency beyond what is currently available in doctrine, and to identify some of the corresponding implications for agencies which are part of the reconstruction effort, especially the Army, a tabletop war game was conducted over a 1-month period in the spring of 2009. Participants were solicited based on their knowledge of and experience in the key agencies involved in past and likely future reconstruction operations. The author acted as the moderator and exercise director, and was assisted in this effort by the U.S. Army Peacekeeping and Stability Operations Institute.[1]

The exercise was conducted in five "turns": Turn 1, Receipt of a basic scenario and analysis by participants; Turn 2, Identification of the key reconstruction tasks; Turn 3, Identification of responsibilities for key tasks, by agency; Turn 4, Matching capabilities to tasks, identifying shortfalls, discussion of possible ways to address a shortfall in capability; and Turn 5, Collection of feedback from participants, and moderator questions and follow up based on review of all input; and issue identification.

THE SCENARIO

To generate feedback from player agencies, a base scenario was designed that described conditions in a nation typical of those found by the United States in past COIN and related operations, and which are likely to be similar to those that will be encountered during future operations.[2]

Country X is an underdeveloped nation that has recently emerged from a period of significant civil strife. A new government has been installed to carry the nation into upcoming democratic elections, which will be the first in the nation's history. Country X is generally at peace with its neighbors; there is no significant threat of outside intervention or attack from across the nation's boundaries. The interim government and all major political parties are viewed by the United States as being friendly and supportive of U.S. interests in the region. The recent history of civil strife has created some immediate and fairly significant humanitarian concerns—small refugee camps have sprung up and are experiencing shortages of food, basic sanitation, and potable water. At present, there is no major presence of international organizations (IOs) or nongovernmental organizations (NGOs) based on security concerns described below.

The political situation in Country X is fairly typical of an underdeveloped nation emerging from a prolonged period of civil strife. Governance at all levels in the nation is weak and largely ineffectual. National ministries are lacking in capability due to the scarcity of experienced government personnel and underdeveloped bureaucracies. There is a noticeable lack of communication between activities and organizations at the national level and between the national government and governments at the provincial level and lower. Despite these facts the national government is cautiously well-received by the people, the majority being willing to wait and see if the government will be able to deliver to meet their basic needs. However, the problem of corruption represents a significant challenge to the legitimacy and acceptability of the government at the national and local level.

Country X is a rural nation whose economy is based primarily on agriculture. The nation has a legacy of central government control of the economy and commercial activities. Agricultural collectives and most major factories are state owned. Civil strife has produced significant disruptions to Country X's economy, aggravated by the damage done to the nation's infrastructure and its poor state of maintenance — systems that support supplies of electricity, potable water, sewage, and transportation (especially roads) are all in need of repair. There have been some initiatives aimed at stimulating growth of small businesses, but, after some early successes, there has been no larger scale push to expand the effort due to a shortage of investment capital from within the nation or from international sources. Government at the national and local levels has proven unable to execute the small budgets that they have developed, revenues for which come mostly from income generated by agricultural exports and donations from abroad, to include IOs and NGOs.

The security situation in Country X is unstable. In the wake of the civil strife that has recently subsided, several small factions that felt disenfranchised by the negotiated solution have started to resist efforts by the central government to extend its reach and domain over the more remote regions of the country, and some groups have taken up arms. Security of Country X's borders against large scale infiltration or armed attack is not a concern, but the national army and police are undermanned, ill equipped, and poorly trained for the purposes of defeating any large-scale armed internal resistance movement or maintaining civil control or order. Corruption is a problem in both the army and the police force. The rule of law is in poor shape. Though a body of established law is in effect, there is no functioning system of jurisprudence, and detention and correctional facilities are overwhelmed and in a bad state of repair and maintenance.

Province Y is one of the most developed provinces in the country, but the nation's larger challenges have not bypassed its population, and the nation's biggest security concerns are focused there. The provincial government's ability to function has been hindered by violence and political isolation from the central government. Armed conflict has resulted in considerable damage to buildings, homes, and religious centers, especially in the smaller towns and villages of Province Y.

There are two ethnic groups in the province. "Reds" make up the bulk of the population, and "Blues" are a minority group located mostly in the north. (Reds and Blues are about equally represented in the population of Country X at large, with the current national government being run by a Red-Blue coalition.). The insurgency got its start in Blueland (an ethnic region that includes a portion of Province Y and spans an international border), and most of the remaining insurgents are Blues or foreign fighters whom they have harbored in their midst. The insurgency is made more complex by the existence of a tribal system which, though weakened by decades of war, is still the dominant structure of governance at levels below the province. Though political party affiliation is loosely tied to tribal affiliation, partisan politics based on ethnic or tribal struggle has not yet become a source of significant strife or violence.

The resistance in Country X, especially in province Y, is taking on the characteristics of a classical insurgency. Opposition forces are beginning to exploit the apparent failures of the central government to deliver essential services to the people. There has been a rise in insurgent attacks on government facilities and, in some cases, public places in an attempt to prove the government's inability to secure the population. Country X's insurgents have begun to appeal to international terrorist organizations for support, and some of these have begun to take credit for a few of the more high profile attacks against the government and people of Country X. Certain portions of the population have become impatient with Country X's inability to effectively address the growing insurgent threat and provide security and basic services for the people. These groups are increasingly unsupportive of the government, and in some cases have begun to aid the insurgency, or at least will not actively work against it. Periodic outbreaks of rioting and several instances of public disorder have started to occur.

Country X has made an appeal to the United States for military intervention to support the new transitional government and facilitate the conduct of elections. Judging that the declining security situation, increasing instability, and growing insurgency are creating the conditions for international extremist groups to gain a foothold and potential sanctuary within Country X, the United States has agreed to provide military forces, supported by capabilities from appropriate government agencies, to launch a COIN campaign as part of a larger international effort that is underway. A U.S. Joint Task Force (JTF) has been established and committed to the Multinational Force (MNF), which is led by a North Atlantic Treaty Organization (NATO) commander. The JTF consists of 2 Army brigades and one U.S. Marine Corps (USMC) Marine Expeditionary Brigade (MEB), plus conventional and special operations enablers. The JTF commander reports to both the MNF commander and the U.S. ambassador to Country X. The U.S. Agency for International Development (USAID) has committed to supporting the operation with development experts and teams. Other civilian agencies have indicated their willingness to send experts, but specific requests have not yet been made by the ambassador. Province Y is the area of operations assigned to the U.S. JTF by the MNF commander. Funding for military operations includes a specific line for a Commander's Emergency Response Program (CERP). Funds have also been approved for USAID programs, and the Department of State (DoS) has been granted funding to support reconstruction projects. These funds will be controlled by a DoS Reconstruction Management Office operating out of the embassy. The U.S. Army Corps of Engineers will support the reconstruction effort by providing assistance with project management.

Working from this basic scenario, the tabletop players were asked to develop the components of a reconstruction plan that would be an integral part of the COIN effort. There was no specific, interactive role to simulate the integration of offensive and defensive combat operations and reconstruction. When such feedback was deemed necessary, it was provided based on the best estimate of the moderator. The tabletop players used the doctrinal definition of reconstruction to support their actions and deliberations: "The process of rebuilding degraded, damaged, or destroyed political, socioeconomic, and physical infrastructure of a country or territory to create the foundation for long-term development."[3]

Through their game play and feedback, they provided insights and analysis about some of the key factors related to reconstruction and COIN, the requirements that the JTF would face, capabilities to meet those requirements, and the best way to match the two. The participants' observations came back repeatedly to the most pressing matters that practitioners of reconstruction in COIN face—the specific challenges and tasks, responsibilities for these tasks, approaches to accomplishing tasks, capability shortfalls, and key issues that face the various agencies involved in a reconstruction effort, individually and collectively. The following observations, findings, and corresponding implications for the interagency community, with a focus on the Army as a critical player in that community, emerged from the exercise.

OBSERVATIONS

Discussion of Key Tasks, Priorities, and Responsibilities.

There is very little disagreement between the respective players about the reconstruction tasks that face the JTF in Country X. The tasks that they identify are very similar to the inventory found in the new FM 3.07 or the ones drawn from the more detailed lists found in scholarly studies dedicated specifically to reconstruction.[4] Expressed and described in several different ways, nonetheless the discussion of tasks begins with security and then proceeds to four general categories of reconstruction tasks: public order and rule of law, essential services, economic development, and governance. The discussion below captures many of the salient points raised by game participants about the nature of the tasks themselves, assigning them a priority, how they might be sequenced in a COIN campaign plan, and how and by whom the tasks might be accomplished. As would be expected, though there is general agreement on which tasks will need to be addressed, there are differences of opinion on other matters, largely because of the diversity of the group and the different agencies represented.

Security. These are universally seen as first-order tasks that must be accomplished to suppress or reduce levels of violence and restore stability, at least in the near term, for effective reconstruction to proceed. Players view the ability to establish a stable environment across Country X or at least in Province Y as being ideal, but if that proves impossible, then a coordinated effort between reconstruction and military operations in order to secure areas that will be the focus of the first reconstruction efforts should be undertaken. Security is generally viewed by both the military and civilian players as being a prerequisite for successful reconstruction, but, consistent with what has been observed in Iraq and Afghanistan, there are different ideas about when to initiate reconstruction projects that depend on the different views of how security and reconstruction are best integrated to achieve desired effects.

The military players generally press for early initiation of reconstruction tasks, seeing them as being a key step to achieving security itself. The comment is made by a former battalion commander that certain reconstruction activities, if effective, could "get them to stop shooting at our guys."[5] Therefore, military players place a high priority on those tasks that can be initiated in Province Y early on to win hearts and minds and support combat operations to defeat the insurgents—even if that means that the vast majority of those tasks will need to be accomplished by the military forces themselves.

Understandably, civilian agencies are wary of any early large scale reconstruction given the unstable environment in Province Y, and also leery of any reconstruction that might be attempted too hastily. These agencies, especially USAID, place a higher emphasis on early efforts to understand the problems facing the government of Country X that, in turn, are feeding the insurgency. They encourage early conduct of such actions as surveys, interviews, and engagements with the local population in order to understand the fundamental problems before attempting to solve them. The concern is that reconstruction that is not informed by an understanding of the sources of violence will be wasteful, or worse, counterproductive to the overall U.S. effort in Country X.

Public Order and the Rule of Law. This category includes tasks associated with public safety and control, order, and the ability to enforce the law; that is, make arrests, detain those who are suspected to have broken the law, try them in accordance with a generally recognized and respected body of laws, carry out punishments, and accomplish all of this in an environment free of intimidation, coercion, or corruption. Again, all players agree that, after security, the establishment of public order and the rule of law is critical to further reconstruction efforts. But, given the state of development and the turmoil associated with the recent civil conflict in Country X, this is viewed by players as a most difficult set of tasks to accomplish, requiring time and a wide range of skills and knowledge that in most cases is very specific to that country. It was observed that there is no one department in the U.S. Government that is particularly well-suited or positioned to take on these tasks. Players expressed some concern based on past personal experience that, when multiple agencies have been called upon to address these tasks, mostly ad hoc approaches will be attempted in Country X, and they will bring only very limited successes.

Essential Services, Public Utilities, and Infrastructure. There is a strong sense that immediate needs of the local population like these must be identified and addressed as a first order of business — electricity, clean water, sewage, and other necessities that will support at least a marginal standard of living and reasonable public health in Country X, or at least in Province Y. Military players point out that, especially in this area, the ability to bring relief to the suffering of the indigenous population by addressing these needs will have a strong positive influence on efforts to win over the population and gain their cooperation as counterinsurgency operations are conducted — or at least be a factor that might prevent the local people from supporting the insurgency. Public works projects are also viewed as being a large source of employment for military aged males, providing them with a source of income and drawing them away from the ranks of the insurgents.

Other players, especially the former district commanders from the U.S. Army Corps of Engineers who all have extensive experience with the reconstruction of infrastructure in COIN, cautioned that an enduring solution to the challenge of providing essential services, though clearly a desirable goal, might not be a feasible way to win hearts and minds in the near term. The lack of essential services in Country X is connected to a national infrastructure that will require extensive rebuilding, which entails large, time consuming projects, requiring technical expertise, that generally do not lend themselves readily to the employment of large numbers of unskilled indigenous workers. Additionally, these projects will place additional demands on the security and police forces of Country X and the JTF forces since they provide a very lucrative target for sabotage and insurgent attack. Some players note that quickly emplaced temporary measures (for example, portable generators or bottled water) might be attempted in lieu of undertaking the demands of a longer term more enduring solution, at least in the initial stages of the counterinsurgency.

Economic Development. Viewed as perhaps the major cause of discontent among the population of Country X and one of the most critical structural issues needing early attention, players have varying views about which of the primary components of economic development should take priority, given limited relevant resources available to the U.S. JTF. Many view programs dedicated to generating jobs in Province Y as being the top priority for agencies dedicated to economic development, USAID being considered the principal organization with this type of capability. But there is general recognition that most of this type of work will have only a marginal effect on lasting development goals in Country X. Nonetheless, trash pickup, quick fix projects, extensive use of manual labor in public works efforts and the like are viewed as being critical, especially by the military players, to win the support of the population and provide employment to fighting age males who might otherwise find a ready source of income by joining the insurgency. CERP funding (discussed later) is viewed as perhaps the quickest way to fund these activities, and doing so is viewed by all as an appropriate use of such monies.

However, there is also a generally recognized need to undertake more fundamental economic reform and financial and monetary measures that might address the root economic causes of the violence in Country X. Microloans and microgrants at the local level to start up small businesses, especially those in the agricultural sector, are suggested as ways to get economic activity going rapidly. Providing seeds for fast growing crops or technical and medical assistance to families that are raising animals in Province Y can set the conditions for more extensive agricultural and perhaps other business development as the security situation improves. Players view a need for an effort to attract international investment to Country X while recognizing that interest will depend on the ability to establish a stable and relatively secure environment for that investment.

Finally, there are cautions expressed by several players that early efforts at job creation and economic revitalization, designed to generate employment and win hearts and minds quickly, should not be undertaken at cross purposes with or at the expense of necessary longer-term economic projects. Players recommend making careful choices about "make-work" type projects which, though successful in the effort to generate temporary employment, might ultimately divert necessary resources from activities that could bring longer-term benefits in terms of both development objectives and enduring jobs. An example might be the choice involving starting labor-intensive "last mile" electricity projects (repairing the wiring and putting in connections to households) undertaken in a town located in Province Y without careful consideration given to the state of infrastructure repair at large in Country X. Though such a project might well employ military age males, if undertaken without regard for the broader economic development plan, the results might be not only be wasteful but could have the effects of diverting resources needed to bring electricity to an economic development zone built around businesses and industry that will need electricity to operate in another part of Province Y.

Governance. Successful coalition efforts to meet the above needs will not be enough. There is general agreement that the COIN effort will ultimately fail unless the basic needs of the people are being met by the governments of Country X and Province Y. Participants also agree that the first efforts to establish good governance in Province Y and at subprovincial levels should be a bottom up effort—the initial focus being on the mechanisms of government closest to the people, but that this bottom up approach should not be at the expense of the credibility of the central government of Country X. The risk of this effect is definitely present in Province Y. Efforts to improve governance in the province might well have the effect of winning loyalty for local governments while building animosity for the central government of Country X, given the lack of experience and ineffectiveness of the ministries of the central government. The need to convince the population that their government can deliver for them and is worthy of their trust and confidence is viewed as being essential to the overall effort. Of course, the challenge faced by the coalition is a well-known one: The government in Country X actually *cannot* deliver for the people (it lacks the capacity and the reach to do so) and in many ways the central government *does not* deserve the trust and confidence of the people (being largely ineffectual and corrupt).

The required solution—to "build good governance"—seems problematic to players on many levels. First, military units which will generally be the first to feel the effects of inadequate governance (a disgruntled population produces fuel for the insurgency) have very little resident expertise or familiarity with how to establish the instrumentalities of good government. Agencies that do have such experience (for example, USAID) note that the security conditions required to execute their governance programs must permit a certain freedom of action and movement, and they understandably have concerns about the safety of their personnel.

RELATED CONCLUSIONS

1. Players point out that at several points, but especially early in the operation, there is a need to have more information so as to make intelligent choices about the reconstruction effort. Part of this lack of information can be attributed to imperfections in the description of the scenario that was provided. But some of these requests for more information indicated the types of information that key agencies must have before they begin a reconstruction mission in regions affected by insecurity and instability. This observation supports the need for maintaining information on political, economic, and social factors that will affect reconstruction efforts in select nations, or developing an early-entry capability to gather such information as a first order of business. One player suggests the deployment of reconstruction survey teams or "scouts" who are tasked to answer questions or collect information that will support the work of other agencies or organizations arriving in Country X later in the deployment flow.

2. The difficult nature of these tasks and the need to approach them in a coherent and coordinated way raises the issue of organizing the reconstruction effort. Though there is general agreement among the players on *what* needs to be accomplished, there is a general recognition that there will be disagreements on *how* to accomplish these tasks — establishing priorities, sequencing tasks, assigning responsibilities, assessment measures, and the like. This problem manifests itself on two levels — at the theater (Province Y) level where the challenges are mostly about management of the effort, and at the tactical (subprovincial or local) level where the biggest issues concern execution.

The utility of having some set of standard practices or a template for master planning or managing the conduct of national reconstruction to guide the interagency effort in Country X is noted. Players comment that the problem is exacerbated because the contributions of international and nongovernmental organizations will be difficult to account for, as will the contributions to be made by host nation activities in Country X.

At the local level, there is a need for a mechanism to execute the reconstruction effort. The lack of any standard approach to coordinating reconstruction efforts at the tactical or local level in Province Y limits the ability of commanders, development experts, and others involved in the effort to maintain visibility, monitor, or assess the work that is being done overall by the various activities in the province. There is also no means to ensure that efforts are mutually reinforcing, or, at least, deconflicted. It follows naturally that synchronizing the reconstruction effort with the security operations of military forces becomes very difficult.

3. Likewise, in terms of the reconstruction effort in Country X writ large, all players note that there is no indication of organizations, U.S. or coalition, that have been established specifically to manage the reconstruction effort at the national level, a condition which is generally consistent with their experiences in actual theaters of operation. Thus, the matter of overall coordination of the component activities of the reconstruction effort in Country X will be problematic.

Players indicate that organizing for the planning and management of reconstruction in Country X will need to be considered on at least three levels: first, at a policy level, most likely in Washington where the overall strategy for reconstruction of Country X would be planned, priorities established, and resources made available; second, at the theater level, where the JTF commander's campaign plan should be synchronized with the objectives of the reconstruction effort ongoing in Country X; and third, at the level of execution, where tactical units and reconstruction agencies will be required to collaborate on priorities, establish mutually supporting local or tactical objectives for the area, and support each other in the management of key projects.

Naturally, given these requirements for coordination, the issue of "who will be in charge?" comes up regularly. Beyond the broad guidance in NSPD-44 which gives the Secretary of State the policy lead for reconstruction and stabilization, there is a need for clarity about who will make decisions, give guidance and direction, and set priorities for interagency reconstruction activities in Country X.

4. There is significant agreement that reconstruction efforts need to be organized around two central purposes related to counterinsurgency—first, to win

hearts and minds by providing for the needs of the population, thus demonstrating that cooperation with the coalition (identified, as it must be, as supporting the central government of Country X) will bring advantages to the people that the insurgents will not be able to provide; and second, to address fundamental structural and developmental problems of national and local government, the economy, rule of law, national infrastructure systems, and other issues that are giving the insurgents a cause upon which to build support for their efforts. Players generally concur that in Country X and Province Y addressing these fundamental problems should be the province of the civilian agencies with expertise in the various areas of development. But some players (mostly military) express doubt that these agencies will be able to act quickly enough to affect the course of the COIN in its early stages. Therefore, military players, especially those with a civil affairs background, are inclined to advocate for military units to undertake some of the longer term, capacity building activities (especially at the local level) even while acknowledging that the comparative advantage in these areas rests with civilian agencies.

The tradeoff between the need to demonstrate that the government is delivering for the people and the time sensitivity of showing progress in the near term, especially at the local level, is of concern to the players, especially given the relative inexperience of the national and local governments and their respective bureaucracies. This tradeoff also carries over to discussion of the relative importance of two key groups of tasks — those that can be executed quickly, are high profile, and are designed primarily to highlight the government's ability to deliver by making efforts to "put the Country X face on it," and the longer term, more enduring capacity building effort, whereby institutions are built and strengthened so that the government is able to sustain its performance over a period of time. Ideally, capacity building can start early and progress quickly so that the governments of Country X and Province Y can begin to perform and provide for their population; in practice, capacity building has been difficult to execute. So there will be a strong inclination for the JTF in Province Y to focus on highly visible, short-term reconstruction work, ideally assisting from a standpoint that allows them to remain "over the horizon." Capacity building activities followed by host nation management of projects and programs is likely to be a lesser priority in the early stages of the mission.

5. There is also a sense that, given the relative advantages that Province Y has over other portions of Country X and the potential benefits that will accrue to the deployment of a large U.S. contingent, reconstruction, development and reform within the province might be realized more quickly than at the national level. This could have a salutary effect on progress throughout Country X if Province Y is viewed as a model to be emulated elsewhere in the nation. But there is also a chance that the disparity could become an additional source of conflict if the effects are not managed carefully. Additionally, trying to drive the reconstruction effort in Country X from the bottom up runs the risk of bolstering the support of Province Y's population for their local leaders at the expense of the credibility and perception of the central government.

6. Military and civilian players note that they have a good understanding of the capabilities of other agencies involved in reconstruction, and thus they can

make certain calculations about their requirements based on their knowledge of others' likely contributions. But many note that they (the players) are experienced practitioners of reconstruction, and that the resident knowledge in their agencies or units (especially in the military) does not support accurate assessments of the likely needs of other agencies or the capabilities that they bring to the effort that might be leveraged. For example, Army units entering an area of operations in Province Y are well versed in what tasks they need to accomplish to conduct counterinsurgency operations. But they might not be aware that the USAID teams that will be working in the same area have information requirements that, if filled beforehand, will facilitate the work of USAID once their personnel are able to enter the province and begin work. Civilian agencies view the military as having the greatest ability to shape the course of the reconstruction effort initially, owing to their greater ability to operate right away under the security conditions as they stand, their ample resources, and the flexibility with which they can employ them (especially CERP money). Military players generally overestimate the resources available to civilian agencies for reconstruction, and opinions in the military about the flexibility of the CERP program tend to vary based on the experiences of the individual player providing the observation.

7. All players note the importance of coordinating the coalition's reconstruction work with that of IOs and NGOs that are present in Country X, but generally feel that it is not reasonable to expect extensive cooperation from or coordination with these organizations, especially when it comes to activities that can be perceived as work that they are doing with the U.S. military. Players from the U.S. civilian agencies

who have standing relationships with IOs and NGOs observe that this fact must also be a consideration in how they do business with the military, lest identification of the agencies of the U.S. Government with coalition military interfere with their ability to work with NGOs or IOs.

8. Several players, especially those with experience working with USAID, note that Country X in general and Province Y specifically might well benefit from the involvement of private enterprise in the areas of investment, economic revitalization, and development. One player suggests that U.S. private businesses might be convinced to support a broader effort to promote economic activity in Country X, an approach that has been attempted in both Iraq and Afghanistan with mixed results. These players point to the desirability of having some organization or mechanism that can be included as part of the coalition's overall reconstruction effort that is charged specifically with facilitating contacts between U.S. business and financial concerns and the appropriate entities within Country X.

9. Though not specifically treated in the scenario, players express concern about measures of effectiveness, based on the lack of any mention of them in the narrative and on experience they have had with them in Afghanistan and Iraq. The first order issue is establishing a useful relationship between these measures and actual progress on the ground in the reconstruction and security arena in a way that tells the leaders of the JTF something about progress towards overall campaign goals. Another issue is reconciling measures of effectiveness and milestones being tracked by the JTF with those most important to Country X. Given certain conditions described in the scenario, it is anticipated that the two may not coincide.

Taken with the observations drawn from a review of the history of reconstruction in counterinsurgency operations and a review of current doctrine, these insights from the tabletop exercise and the conclusions that flow from them suggest some issue areas that deserve attention in order to enhance the effectiveness of reconstruction in COIN. Some of these areas and certain measures to address them involve the whole of government approach to reconstruction. Any Army initiatives to improve the effectiveness of its contributions to the reconstruction effort must be considered in that context. The next chapter recommends an overall concept of reconstruction that would, if adopted by the interagency community, produce a more coherent and coordinated holistic effort, and allow the Army to consider recommendations, presented in Chapter 6, designed to optimize its contributions to reconstruction in COIN.

ENDNOTES - CHAPTER 4

1. Special thanks for their support of and participation in the exercise goes to Ambassador Joe Saloom (U.S. Department of State); Elena Brineman (USAID); the U.S. Army Peacekeeping and Stability Operations Institute (Colonel John Kardos, Director, along with Thomas Dempsey, Bryan Grover, Richard Megahan, Michael Moon); the Center for a New American Security (John Nagl, President, along with Colonels James Crider and Michael Garrett, who were military fellows at the time of the exercise); and Debra Lewis, Bob Vasta, Ron Light, and Rick Jenkins, all past regional commanders in the Gulf Region Division, Iraq, U.S. Army Corps of Engineers.

2. Some of the conditions described in the scenario used in the exercise are drawn from an early draft of the Nangarhar case study that, in its final form, appears in Chap. 2 of Gompert *et al.*, *Reconstruction Under Fire*. However, the scenario depicts a fictional situation and is not meant to describe circumstances in Nan-

garhar or in Afghanistan. Information from that scenario is used in this monograph by permission of Dr. Kelly. Special thanks to Michelle Parker who is the author of the Nangahar case study in the book.

3. *Field Manual (FM) 3-07, Stability Operations*, Washington, DC: Department of the Army, p. Glossary-9.

4. Conrad Crane and W. Andrew Terrill, *Reconstructing Iraq: Insights, Challenges, and Missions for Military Forces in a Post-Conflict Scenario*, Carlisle, PA: Strategic Studies Institute, U.S. Army War College, February, 2003, especially Appendix A.

5. As quoted in email message to the author.

CHAPTER 5

A FRAMEWORK FOR RECONSTRUCTION IN COUNTERINSURGENCY

To this point, a review of the history of the role that reconstruction has played in warfare since the beginning of the 20th century, a survey of the most current and relevant doctrine and other writings on counterinsurgency (COIN), and the experiences of modern practitioners in ongoing overseas operations makes it possible to draw these conclusions about reconstruction and the role that it plays in COIN warfare:

- First, our conception of what reconstruction is and its role in war has evolved over time. Whereas it has previously been thought of almost exclusively in terms of rebuilding after war has ended, increasingly in the post-World War II period, various U.S. experiences have caused us to view reconstruction as an integral part of war, especially of COIN operations. That said, general acceptance of reconstruction as part of warfare has not been universal. Whereas there have been strong advocates of its importance in an overall COIN effort, there has also been much resistance to "nation building" on the grounds that it takes military forces away from their core responsibilities ("war fighting") and therefore constitutes a form of "mission creep."

- Second, emerging U.S. Army and Joint doctrine is very clear about the critical role that reconstruction plays in successful COIN operations. Current doctrine on Joint and Army operations holds that reconstruction must be considered as at least equal to — if not more important than — other functions or lines of operation in COIN.

- Third, that there is complete agreement across the U.S. Government that reconstruction must be an interagency effort. There is also agreement across agencies about the key tasks that should be included in a reconstruction effort in support of COIN. But as yet there is no clearly stated or agreed upon concept or common framework that can serve as a guide for the key activities of all relevant players from the interagency community to assist in coordinating a whole of government reconstruction effort, and integrating it with the other elements of successful COIN.

The U.S. Government has consistently fallen short in its attempts to organize for and implement reconstruction in a way that has led to an effective or efficient use of resources dedicated to that purpose.[1] For that reason, reconstruction has had a suboptimal impact in COIN campaigns undertaken by the United States. It is difficult to estimate how far short of the mark the effort has fallen because there is also no clear set of established measures that have been used to account for the contribution that reconstruction has made in U.S. COIN campaigns. But it is hard to argue against some sort of reform or change in the way reconstruction in support of COIN should be managed and conducted. Though most agencies involved in reconstruction are working hard to identify basic principles, offer recommendations on various ways to organize to manage and implement reconstruction, and attempt to collect lessons learned that are mostly drawn from ad hoc approaches attempted in recent COIN operations, this work is proceeding largely in the absence of any agreed upon organizing framework or concept of reconstruction—a fact which threatens to limit the utility of any conclusions that might emerge. It follows that successful integration of reconstruction into Army COIN operations will require more than just internal measures taken to enhance its own ability to contribute to an overall reconstruction effort. The larger, holistic framework for whole of government reconstruction must continue to evolve and develop.

THE FRAMEWORK: A CONCEPT FOR RECONSTRUCTION

An agreed upon concept of reconstruction to guide planning, preparation for, and execution of reconstruction operations in support of COIN will be of great benefit, if not essential, to this evolution. Such a concept could guide the actions of all participating agencies in order that they be coordinated and synchronized in support of an overall COIN campaign plan. The operational concept should include the following five components:

1. A statement of the purpose of reconstruction;
2. A description of the essential elements;
3. A general sequence/scheme of reconstruction activities;
4. Guidelines for assigning responsibilities;
5. Guidelines for assessment of a reconstruction effort.

An outline of a concept that treats these components can be drawn from a study of history, existing directives, current doctrine, relevant studies, and the work of various agencies and organizations that are studying the attendant issues. The following discussion draws from many such sources, compiling this work, and drawing logical conclusions from some of the best thinking being done on reconstruction to posit a form of framework for reconstruction that will be relevant to all departments and agencies. Naturally, if adopted, this concept will have implications for the Army's doctrine, organization, training, and equipment. These implications are the subject of Chapter 6.

Purpose of Reconstruction.

Building the concept proceeds from the previous discussion of the two purposes of reconstruction, which, though they are related, must be considered as distinct, a premise which has profound impact on further development of a concept.

The first purpose of reconstruction is to provide incentives to the local population to support the counterinsurgent and withdraw their support from the insurgent. This will be accomplished if reconstruction projects and programs are viewed as attractive to the population or meeting some immediate need, and that cooperation with the counterinsurgent will bring more of the same, or alternatively, that failure to cooperate will bring an end to the benefit being received. Actions to this end are normally time and conditions sensitive, and their effectiveness is directly proportional to the ability of the population to identify the benefits with the counterinsurgent force. In short, reconstruction must *win the hearts and minds of the population.*

The second purpose of reconstruction is to address the fundamental sources of instability or discontent that are the incipient cause of the insurgency itself. This will generally be accomplished by addressing certain failures of legitimate governments or other authorities to provide for the basic needs of the population and will necessarily involve programs of capacity building or reform that are inherently longer-term efforts, requiring the expertise of functional experts or mentors. As capacity grows and the needs of the people are more regularly and consistently met, the legitimacy of the host nation government in the eyes of the population increases, and support for that government grows. Fulfilling this second purpose of reconstruction requires the counterinsurgent coalition to lead a *nation building* effort.

Essential Elements of Reconstruction.

An analyst can go to any one of several sources to find discussions of the elements of reconstruction, which is part of the challenge in arriving at a consensus on what exactly reconstruction is. Beyond just the need for conceptual clarity, a commonly accepted understanding of the essential elements of reconstruction—one that is best distilled from these sources—is called for before key decisions about an executable concept, responsibilities, and resourcing can be developed:

- It is useful to begin with *National Security Presidential Directive (NSPD) 44*, which provides guidance to the interagency community on the management of reconstruction and stabilization, and lists the component elements as being activities designed "to promote peace, security, development, democratic practices, market economies, and the rule of law."[2]
- The *U.S. Government Counterinsurgency Guide* was developed by the Bureau of Political-Military Affairs in the Department of State, co-signed by the Secretaries of Defense and

State and the Administrator of the U.S. Agency for International Development (USAID), and released in January 2009. Though mostly descriptive of the characteristics of insurgency and COIN, it is the only document approved by these three departments that treats the elements of reconstruction. In what is portrayed as "a comprehensive approach to COIN," the guide describes two "imperatives" — political ("the key function" in COIN) and security — both of which must be addressed with "equal urgency." Three other "components of COIN" are included in the formulation — economic, information, and control.[3]

- *DoD Directive (DoDD) 3000.05, Military Support for Stability, Security, Transition, and Reconstruction (SSTR) Operations,* describes reconstruction as follows: "The immediate goal often is to provide the local populace with security, restore essential services, and meet humanitarian needs. The long-term goal is to help develop indigenous capacity for securing essential services, a viable market economy, rule of law, democratic institutions, and a robust civil society."[4]

- *Field Manual (FM) 3-0, Operations,* describes stability operations (as a component of full spectrum operations) in Chapter 3 and presents a crosswalk of "stability tasks" as described in military doctrine (establish civil security, establish civil control, restore essential services, support to governance, support to economic and infrastructure development) with the "post-conflict reconstruction and stabilization sectors" that are recognized by the Department of State (security, justice and reconciliation, humanitarian assistance and social well-being, governance and participation, economic stabilization and infrastructure).[5]

- As previously cited, the glossary of *Field Manual (FM) 3-07, Stability Operations,* defines reconstruction as "the process of rebuilding degraded, damaged, or destroyed political socioeconomic, and physical infrastructure of a country or territory to create the foundation for long term development."[6] Since FM 3-07 is the "proponent manual" for this definition, it stands for all Services in the Department of Defense (DoD).

- *Field Manual (FM) 3-24, Counterinsurgency,* makes mention of reconstruction in numerous places, but provides no definition and does not include a separate list of what constitutes reconstruction tasks.

- There are various professional studies that include detailed discussions of reconstruction tasks. One of the best is a thesis published by the Strategic Studies Institute of the U.S. Army War College and written by Dr. Conrad Crane and Dr. W. Andrew Terrill entitled *Reconstructing Iraq: Insights, Challenges, and Missions for Military Forces in a Post-Conflict World.* In an appendix to this monograph, the authors provide a "mission task matrix" that is broken down into 21 categories of "essential missions that must be performed to maintain a viable state and change the regime [in Iraq]."[7] Though the monograph is focused on the war in Iraq, it is possible to generalize from the subset of reconstruction tasks that the authors provide and draw on them for the purposes of this discussion of COIN. The full range of tasks in this monograph is connected to phases of overseas military intervention that run from decisive operations through transition. Their listing of reconstruction tasks are grouped mostly into four categories — establish security, stabilize, build institutions, and hand over.

A hard and fast definition of reconstruction that is based on a specific set list of tasks is neither possible nor desirable. The goal of establishing a concept of reconstruction should be to clarify without too much specificity and gain a common understanding that can be accepted and used for planning and preparing for as well as execution of reconstruction activities, while at the same time avoiding description that is so broad that it provides no help. Therefore, reviewing the discussions contained in the aforementioned sources, it seems that reconstruction tasks might best be thought of in terms of *two basic elements of reconstruction that are related to its purposes*:

The first element consists of those tasks that are focused on meeting the immediate needs of the population, to win their support and preclude the possibility of insurgents taking advantage of grievances associated with basic needs in order to bolster their cause or make them an accelerant of the insurgency. The primary focus of such tasks is the population. They have to do with those needs that are immediate and pressing, and they are generally easy to identify and diagnose in the early stages after an intervention. They are also generally best dealt with at the local (as opposed to the national) level.

The second element corresponds to the category of reconstruction tasks generally focused on strengthening legitimate institutions, authorities, or processes and patterns of the host nation. These tasks are focused on fundamental or structural issues—be they the ones having to do with administration or governance, economics or financial activities, public safety and the rule of law, or the like—and generally require an in depth understanding of cultural, social, and political patterns and characteristics of the host nation. They lend themselves only to longer-term efforts to build capacity in the host nation's institutions and are generally best addressed by host nation officials with the assistance of technical experts from the counterinsurgent force.

A Scheme of Reconstruction.

In order to achieve synchronicity of reconstruction activities and integration with other activities that are critical to a successful COIN effort, there should be some agreement between all the agencies about a general sequence that might guide the reconstruction effort. In describing COIN campaigns, FM 3-24 provides the somewhat stark analogy of patient care to describe a general sequence of events or rough stages of a COIN:

- first, stop the bleeding
- then, assist recovery during inpatient care
- finally, bring the patient to self-sufficiency that, in medical terms, occurs during outpatient care.

In their discussion of a mission matrix that can be applied to COIN, Crane and Terrill propose thinking about the transition phase of that war in terms of four steps that are related to reconstruction.[8] These steps should not be viewed as rigidly sequential; in fact, if they are executed that way the effectiveness of the reconstruction effort will likely be undermined. But a general scheme of reconstruction that can serve as a useful guide is derived by making some connections between the mission matrix in the SSI study and the discussion in FM 3-24 as follows:

Stop the Bleeding. Establish security: Offensive operations against the insurgent and other military actions to establish (or restore) stability are the *supported effort.* The reconstruction effort is the *supporting effort,* and it is focused primarily on the population to provide for immediate needs — humanitarian relief, emergency assistance, and restoration of essential services. Quick impact, visible improvements, early wins, and making maximum progress during the "golden hour" (to use another medical analogy) are critical to success in this phase.

In stopping the bleeding, the early stages of an intervention present both opportunities and dangers. In most cases, this is the period characterized by the greatest turmoil, disorder, and often violence. But it is usually also the time when the insurgent has had the least opportunity to exercise control over or influence the majority of the population. Here is when "reconstruction under fire" is most applicable. The ability to attend to the immediate needs of the people in the early stages of a COIN can be decisive. In this stage, while military forces are attacking the insurgents to break their momentum, dismantle their networks, and reduce their ability to threaten the population, the reconstruction effort should best be focused on attending to the immediate needs of the population for civil order, relief, essential services and the like.

Inpatient Care; Stabilize the Patient. Stabilize the situation: The supporting/supported relationship depends on the level of instability that obtains. As military operations shift from offensive actions against the insurgent to securing the population, establishing civil security, and restoring order and authority, the reconstruction is primarily focused on host nation security and governance at the local level (for example, the rule of law and the administration of key government services, especially jobs programs).

Build Institutions. The supported effort is capacity building. The security effort is focused on building military and police institutions and operations to protect the population *and* secure key capacity building activities. The reconstruction effort targets infrastructure, the economic and business sectors, establishment of the rule of law, and then moves to education, medical services, and commerce.

According to FM 3-24, during recovery while in inpatient care, the focus of the overall COIN effort is stability. Combat operations to protect the population continue, but security of reconstruction activities, especially capacity building, is also a priority. Capacity in the security sector is built through training and combined operations and patrolling. Other reconstruction activities build upon efforts undertaken in stage 1 (stop the bleeding) and begin to turn to capacity building activities. Programs are implemented to strengthen governments so that they are able to provide for the needs of the people and are viewed as effective and legitimate. Infrastructure capacity is rebuilt so that temporary efforts to stop the bleeding can be replaced by means that are more permanent and reliable and are run by the host nation. Efforts to restore self-sustaining economic and commercial activities, especially at the local level, are undertaken.

Outpatient Care; Getting the Patient Ready for Discharge. Handover: Both the security and reconstruction efforts are focused on establishing competence, capability, effectiveness, and reach of the legitimate host nation governments and preparing them to take full responsibility for the key functions.

The last stage is movement to self-sufficiency. In this stage, U.S. combat operations are winding down and being turned over to a host nation military that has acquired the capacity to assume the responsibility for conducting them. A concomitant effort on the reconstruction side would see capacity building activities drawing down and responsibilities for key activities being turned over to strengthened local and national institutions. Training for maintenance and operations, and other activities that support a smooth transition to host nation responsibility are a priority.

Responsibilities.

This component of a concept for reconstruction in support of COIN has been the topic of much acrimonious debate. This is especially true when discussions turn to which tasks are inherently military and which should be the responsibility of civilian agencies. Of course, there are also disagreements between individual civilian agencies about the allocation of responsibility for specific tasks among them, but that matter is beyond the scope of this chapter. Finally, there are often disagreements among agencies about which tasks should be left to the host nation and when the host nation should assume those tasks.

Any discussion of responsibilities must begin with the relevant guidance that is contained in national directives. NSPD 44 states clearly that:

The Secretary of State shall coordinate and lead integrated United States Government efforts, involving all U.S. Departments and Agencies with relevant capabilities, to prepare, plan for, and conduct stabilization and reconstruction activities. The Secretary of State shall coordinate such efforts with the Secretary of Defense to ensure harmonization with any planned or ongoing U.S. military operations across the spectrum of conflict.[9]

And later that:

The Secretaries of State and Defense will integrate stabilization and reconstruction contingency plans with military contingency plans when relevant and appropriate. The Secretaries of State and Defense will develop a general framework for fully coordinating stabilization and reconstruction activities and military operations at all levels where appropriate.[10]

Drawing from the NSPD, DoDD 3000.05 provides guidance that is taken to implement the operative provisions of NSPD-44 for the DoD. Its purpose is described as "[to establish] DoD policy and assign responsibilities within the Department of Defense for planning, training, and preparing to conduct and support stability operations pursuant to the authority vested in the Secretary of Defense."[11] Though the directive is entitled "Military Support for Stability, Security, Transition, and Reconstruction (SSTR) Operations," the following key paragraph in DoDD 3000.05 seems to indicate that the responsibilities of the military will at times go well beyond support:

Many stability operations tasks are best performed by indigenous, foreign, or U.S. civilian professionals. Nonetheless, U.S. military forces shall be prepared to perform all tasks necessary to establish or maintain order when civilians cannot do so.[12]

If this guidance is to be interpreted literally, then U.S. military forces entering COIN operations today are not prepared to meet the demands of reconstruction in COIN, and it is inconceivable that they ever will be able to be so prepared. A realistic guide to the readiness of military units for reconstruction in COIN can be based on the following principles:

- Military reconstruction efforts are most usefully focused on attending to immediate needs that support wining the hearts of minds of the population and that will facilitate combat operations against the insurgent.
- Concurrently, even before civilian agencies are able to fully implement reconstruction programs, the military must focus on reconstruction tasks that will set the conditions for success of these civilian agencies. Many of these tasks will be related to gathering and managing key information that will be essential to the success of subsequent civilian efforts. Therefore, close coordination with those agencies whose efforts will follow is essential.
- The military has very little experience with or expertise in most tasks associated with capacity building of host nation civilian institutions. Rebuilding or strengthening these institutions consists of mostly civilian tasks and should be left to civilian agencies. The primary military responsibility in this area will be to secure the effort, which implies that commanders understand the manner in which civilian agencies carry out capacity building and other related reconstruction activities.
- Notwithstanding the desire to put responsibility for reconstruction goals into the hands of

the host nation (or put a "host nation face" on them), doing so should be a lower priority than gaining and keeping the support of the population through a successful reconstruction effort, especially in the early stages of COIN. U.S. civilian and military activities must coordinate closely in the effort to pass responsibility for accomplishing critical reconstruction objectives to the host nation.

Assessment.

The final element of a concept for reconstruction is assessment. The weaknesses of current assessment regimes that have been relied upon in order to measure effectiveness have received enormous scrutiny, especially in Congress—which is to be expected given that the ongoing reconstruction efforts in Afghanistan and Iraq account for billions of dollars of appropriated funds. Beyond the need to ensure that valuable resources are being put to good use, accurate assessment of the effectiveness of a reconstruction effort in support of COIN is a critical contributing factor to successful execution. The ability to gauge the relative impact of different reconstruction activities and make timely adjustments is critical to effective COIN, just as the ability to adjust indirect fires can be critical to successful maneuver.

The most fundamental challenge has been to decide what exactly to measure. The simplest approach has been to measure inputs—resources that are being dedicated to the reconstruction effort. Input measures have been much maligned, but are still relied on heavily because data to support them is the most reliable and readily available. And it is not inconsequential to know what portion of resources made available is actually being put to use, when and at what rate, and where the specific areas of focus are.

Output measures have also been relied upon to gauge the progress of reconstruction. The number and types of projects started and completed, time to complete, number of persons trained or graduated from various educational programs, and other similar measures also have some utility, especially in measuring efficiency or the return on resources expended.

Universally acclaimed as the most desirable assessment methods are those that measure outcomes in terms of the desired *effects* of reconstruction programs. The most sought after of these are the ones that provide insight on effects that are tied to overall campaign goals, that is, the progress of the COIN itself. There has often been disagreement on which indicators are the most relevant to this purpose. Military organizations tend to judge the outcome of reconstruction efforts based on the effect on levels of violence, number of attacks, and other indicators of insurgent activity. Civilian agencies prefer to use survey techniques and methods to measure the satisfaction of the population with their living conditions and with the institutions of national governance.

In his study "Measuring Progress in International State Building and Reconstruction," Rick Barton from the Center for Strategic and International Studies (CSIS) advocates a deliberate review of current assessment regimes.[13] He notes that existing programs lack even the basic essential elements that will yield meaningful measures of progress — clearly established baselines, mechanisms that will allow for the measurement of trends, and relevant capabilities to gather data and information being the most important. His approach argues for assessment that is based on a mix of input, output, and outcome measures and accompanying methods to support their collection. Most importantly, he provides examples that have proven useful in tracking progress in Iraq and Afghanistan that are based on trends and the movements of a few key variables in those counterinsurgencies over time.

A last thought: Measurement of progress of reconstruction in COIN must be tied closely to the two distinct purposes of the effort—that is, gaining the support of the population for the counterinsurgent and addressing the fundamental causes of the insurgency. Measures that correlate to progress in the first are more likely to be outcome measures that gauge the degree to which hearts and minds are being won. Output measures of capacity building efforts addressing fundamental causes of the insurgence, such as increases in productivity and effectiveness (or lack thereof) in targeted national institutions and organizations, should not be dismissed out of hand in favor of attempts to find outcome measures in this area, which are elusive and often lack relevance. Counterinsurgent coalitions that have the capability to compare various reconstruction courses of action in terms of the positive effects achieved in both areas, and incorporate those assessments in their planning, will be more likely to plan, prepare for, and execute more effective COIN campaigns.

ORGANIZING AND MANAGING THE RECONSTRUCTION EFFORT

In COIN, perhaps more so than in any other type of full spectrum operation, success depends on the ability to tailor execution to the specific conditions encountered in the area of operations. Therefore the organization of the instrumentalities of control and management of the important actions in COIN is key. Design that permits flexibility, quick adjustment, and responsiveness without sacrificing unity of effort, co-ordinated and coherent execution, and the ability to integrate all the capabilities inherent in the counterinsurgent coalition to the greatest effect is the ideal.

Given the number of players involved, the characteristics of the operational environment, differing views on the core purpose of the reconstruction effort and the role it should play in COIN, and the wide range of tasks associated with these purposes, it is no surprise that management has been a huge challenge. This situation has not been made any easier by the fact that, with the exception of the institution of one or two transitory and usually ad hoc arrangements, there has never been an established controlling authority to manage or execute reconstruction in COIN. The lack of any established structure for managing a reconstruction effort has led to confusion, a lack of coordination, friction, and disagreement over approach that has been evident in recent experiences in reconstruction efforts that are part of the wars in Iraq and Afghanistan. Multiple tales of waste, duplication of effort, bureaucratic infighting, and general ineffectiveness in the reconstruction efforts in Iraq and Afghanistan are well-documented.[14] Many of these problems could be addressed if there was an established reconstruction architecture to manage the effort at three critical levels.

ORGANIZING THE U.S. GOVERNMENT FOR RECONSTRUCTION IN COIN OPERATIONS: THE POLICY LEVEL

Much has been written and numerous studies have been undertaken to review how the U.S. Government should organize for stabilization and reconstruction operations such as those that would be undertaken as part of COIN. The fundamental weakness at the level of the U.S. Government that currently stands in the way of conducting coordinated reconstruction efforts in COIN is the lack of any effective body that has the capability to "lead, coordinate and institutionalize U.S. Government civilian capacity to prevent or prepare for post-conflict situations, and to help stabilize and reconstruct societies in transition from conflict or civil strife"—which is in fact a quote taken from the mission statement of the State Department's Office of the Coordinator for Reconstruction and Stabilization (S/CRS).[15] It is interesting to note that, despite the fact that the Department of State has been directed in NSPD-44 to lead the interagency effort, and DoDD 3000.05 acknowledges that role, the mission statement for S/CRS mentions coordination of only "civilian capacity."[16]

Of course, S/CRS could never aspire to manage a reconstruction effort from Washington. But it could ensure that the policies of the agencies that participate in reconstruction are harmonized, that procedures that they employ are consistent, and that the departments maintain the capabilities required to meet the requirements to support overseas operations such as the two COIN missions that the United States finds itself in today. Working closely with the DoD, this type of organization could also play a key role in the interagency planning process as the nation prepares for possible contingencies throughout the world.

Established in 2004 to create a more robust capability within the U.S. Government to prevent conflict when possible, and if necessary manage stabilization and reconstruction operations in countries emerging from conflict or civil strife, S/CRS has languished in the Department of State ever since. It has experienced chronic problems of staffing, resourcing, and inattention, ensuring that to date it has not been able to even come close to meeting its ambitious mission statement or stated objectives.

S/CRS has also been assigned a key role in resourcing reconstruction efforts that, if realized, could prove to be the most important steps taken in Washington to improve reconstruction in COIN. The lack of experienced, qualified, rapidly deployable civilian experts has ensured that reconstruction in COIN will fall short of the mark. In both the 2006 National Security Strategy and his 2007 State of the Union address, President George W. Bush called for the creation of a civilian response corps (CRC) — a sort of equivalent of the military reserves — to help fill the serious gap in the U.S. Government's civilian reconstruction and stabilization capacity.[17]

Since that time, and continuing during the Obama administration, some initial steps have been taken to stand up the CRC. But until full funding and other support can be achieved, an ability to execute the rapid deployment or surge of civilian reconstruction experts will be severely limited, which will hamper the conduct of reconstruction in COIN operations. Past experiences have proven that the so-called "civilian surges" get going only slowly, are difficult to sustain, and most positions are difficult to fill. When they are filled it is largely by military personnel — generally reservists activated based on specialties acquired in their civilian professions.

ORGANIZING THE RECONSTRUCTION EFFORT IN THE COIN THEATER

Given the number of players involved in stability and reconstruction operations, mounting a coordinated effort in support of a COIN operation would be an extreme challenge even if there were a standard for organizing the reconstruction capabilities in theater. During the U.S. experiment with Civil Operations and Revolutionary Development Support (CORDS) in Vietnam, there was an organizing concept for stabilization operations that actually existed and functioned fairly well. One might assume that reconstruction lessons learned in Vietnam are being applied broadly in COIN today. Sadly, that is not always the case, and currently there are even more actors involved in reconstruction than there were in the days of CORDS.

The organization of CORDS was based on a fully integrated, civil-military structure throughout the Republic of Vietnam in all four corps areas of operation, with a CORDS official serving in the chain of command as a counterpart to the military commander at each level. At the time of MACV Directive 10-12 which directed the establishment of CORDS, Robert Komer was designated a deputy to the force commander, General William Westmoreland, and as such his position in the chain of command nominally carried 4-star authority. At the tactical level, CORDS had provincial and district teams, usually headed by civilians, who coordinated closely with the commanders of U.S. tactical units and with the advisory teams that worked with Army of the Republic of Vietnam (ARVN) units at the division, brigade, and battalion level. This structure of CORDS facilitated internal coordination of the reconstruction effort across the theater, and coordination of the reconstruction effort with combat operations being conducted by United States and ARVN forces. (See Figure 5.1.)

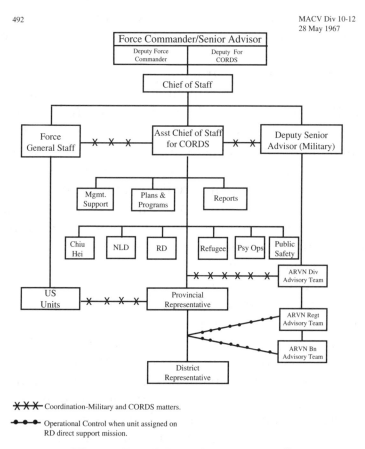

Figure 5.1. CORDS Structure.[18]

There has been no real impetus for adopting a similar integrated structure to manage the reconstruction effort in COIN today. As the results of the war game described in Chapter 4 demonstrated clearly, and consistent with experience in the field, there are numerous civilian agencies performing reconstruction tasks with no mechanism to coordinate their efforts with each other, much less ensuring that they are synchronized with combat operations of either U.S. or host nation forces.

An analog to CORDS would see close linkages between U.S. tactical units, imbedded training teams working with host nation forces, and civilian agencies which are executing the reconstruction program in a COIN environment. However, the coordination that is accomplished in current overseas operations is usually accomplished by means of informal relationships without established systems or procedures—always at the mercy of breakdowns in communications, interagency friction, and interpersonal dynamics.

It is entirely possible, and often occurs, that in the same region tactical military units are conducting combat operations while managing Commander's Emergency Response Program (CERP) projects, at the same time as Army National Guard Agricultural Development Teams are working with local farmers, USAID implementing partners are conducting capacity building programs with local governments, Corps of Engineers project managers are in oversight of contractors who are doing construction for projects requested by various U.S. military units and civilian departments, provincial reconstruction teams are doing quick impact work at the request of the governor, host nation businesses or local governments may be undertaking other efforts, while international organizations (IOs) and nongovernmental organizations (NGOs) are undertaking their missions. Though the chances are fairly good that some of these organizations know what some of the others are doing, there is no mechanism to guarantee that that is the case, and any meaningful coordination is generally just a happy coincidence. And there is certainly no method (or in some cases no desire) to harness these efforts in support of combat operations against insurgents or to protect the population. Given this lack of any structured arrangements to manage the reconstruction effort, there is a huge loss of opportunity to achieve important COIN goals.

This was exactly the case in Iraq when in the summer of 2006 the Multinational Force, Iraq undertook a series of combat operations designed to stabilize Baghdad and check the rising violence in the capital city of 7 million (1/4 of Iraq's population) in an operation that was at first known as the Baghdad Security Plan, later to be called *Fardh al-Qanoon* (roughly "Law and Order"). At the beginning of this operation, the reconstruction effort that was to support combat operations against Al Qaeda in Iraq and win support of the population was disjointed, verging on incoherent. There was no complete, common picture of all the reconstruction projects that were going on in Baghdad at the time of commencement of the campaign (August, 2006). Given the almost complete lack of reconstruction situational awareness, harnessing the reconstruction effort in support of the Baghdad Security Plan was virtually impossible.

In response to the Force Commander's guidance to address this situation, Multinational Corps, Iraq and the Gulf Region Division of the U.S. Army Corps of Engineers devised a system to gain situational awareness and rationalize decisions being made on reconstruction projects in Baghdad in order to ensure that they were tied to the overall COIN campaign there. A Joint Planning Commission (JPC) was established that immediately began to collect data from all agencies and activities that were involved in the reconstruction effort—tactical commanders spending CERP; the Baghdad Provincial Reconstruction Team (PRT) spending Iraq Relief and Reconstruction Fund monies; USAID undertaking several projects and programs to build capacity in Baghdadi infrastructure and local governments; the Army Corps of Engineers Gulf Region Division, Central which was managing several projects requested by various customers; and several others. Iraqi participation in the JPC was initially episodic, but over time it began to grow. Deputy Prime Minister (DPM) Salam Zigum Ali al-Zoubaie participated in JPC meetings, or had representatives with his proxy present at the various proceedings. The *Baghdad Amanat* (roughly a city council) was also represented as were local officials from the various *beladiyahs* (neighborhoods). The JPC compiled a data base that identified all the reconstruction work that was going on in Baghdad at the time and maintained an accurate and current status of each. The Committee also met on a weekly basis to review the data and make recommendations on future work to be undertaken, based on the needs of the local population and synchronized with the combat operations being undertaken by the Multinational Corps, Iraq. The meetings were initially hosted by the Multinational Corp's Effects Manager and the Deputy Director of the Iraq Reconstruction Management Office. Later the meeting was chaired by one of DPM Zoubaie's assistants.

The JPC process made it possible to gain situational awareness of the reconstruction effort as it was being undertaken across Baghdad. Locations of projects and their status, previously unavailable, were now passed to key military and civilian decision makers on a real time basis. Individual agencies and organizations were not bound by the recommendations of the JPC, and, albeit in rare cases, sometimes chose to go their own way on certain projects. A significant shortcoming of the JPC was the absence of a decision support system or assessment mechanism to accurately predict the outcome of specific reconstruction projects, measured against the effects desired by the Ambassador and the Force Commander for their campaign.

In the end the JPC model was never replicated for areas of operation outside of Baghdad and the close-in provinces that were the area of operations of *Fardh al-Qanoon*. No official records of the composition of the JPC or its processes or procedures were ever kept. There is no official document that captures these techniques and procedures employed that might be used as a model for the interagency community or for the military in future operations.[19]

THE LEVEL OF EXECUTION

Finally, and perhaps most critically, is the task of coordination of the execution of a reconstruction effort in support of a COIN at the local or tactical level. It is there where the most critical coordination goes on and where the specific knowledge and understanding of the matters most critical to the reconstruction effort reside. There must be a common understanding among the agencies of who the influencers are, their needs and desires, and what the people need and want. There is also a need to have information on projects and programs and good visibility on how they are supporting each other and being coordinated, what type of progress is being made, and what effects are being achieved. If agencies are operating at the local level in a coordinated fashion and staying abreast of capacity building that is taking place at the national level, there will be opportunities to extend the reach of the central government by mentoring and encouraging local officials to work with the central government to make sure that the needs of their populations are being considered in national decisions.

To this end, during the reconstruction effort that was part of pacification in Vietnam, the organization of CORDS lent itself to just such coordination. The teams at the local level were drawn from the key agencies involved in the development and reconstruction communities. As part of the District Team, they had the ability to work together to ensure that their efforts were coordinated. Additionally, they worked as part of a larger organization, reporting to Provincial Advisors, and as an integrated part of the military chain of command. Though by no means absolute, the authorities of those responsible for reconstruction at the local level were at least linked to the authorities of the Force Commander's Deputy for CORDS, Robert Komer.

Drawing from this CORDS construct there could be an organization designed to bring coherence and integration to interagency efforts to execute reconstruction on the ground in present day COIN operations. It might be built from the existing interagency provincial reconstruction teams that have been established in both Afghanistan and Iraq whose stated purpose is threefold:

1. Increase provincial stability through international military presence and assist in developing nascent host nation security and rule of law capacity.

2. Assist the establishment and improvement of local government, including its connection to the central

government and populace, by advising and empowering stakeholders and legitimate governing bodies, influencing "fence sitters," and countering obstructionists and spoilers.

3. Facilitate reconstruction at a pace that begins to:

- Provide basic services.
- Provide an economic system that supports the people.
- Gain popular buy-in for change and support of representative government.
- Ensure popular expectations for international assistance are met or abated.

In general they are organized as shown in Figure 5.2.

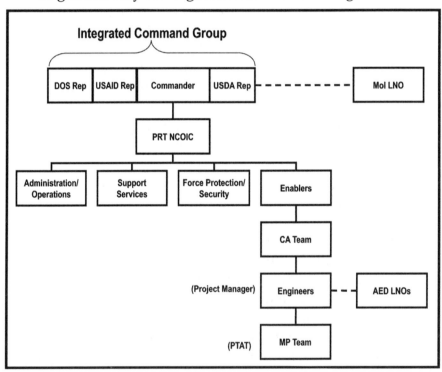

Figure 5.2. PRT Core task organization

The specific purpose of these teams has evolved over time and has never been established in any official document. Even today, in practice each provincial reconstruction team effectively decides for itself what its mandate will be.[21] If agencies of the U.S. Government involved with reconstruction and stabilization activities were to recognize the PRTs as having responsibility for the coordination or integration of reconstruction activities (they do not do so now) and grant them the commensurate authority (which they do not currently have) they could easily become major players in the overall COIN effort.

Recently in Afghanistan, Ambassador Karl Eikenberry has issued guidance that establishes a Senior Civilian Representative (SCR) for Regional Commands East and South. The SCR will act on behalf of the Ambassador and have the responsibility to ". . . coordinate and direct the work of all USG [U.S. Government] civilians under Chief of Mission authority within the region, ensure coherence of political direction and developmental efforts, and execute U.S. policy and guidance."[22] The SCR will have an interagency staff to assist with this mission. This team's primary purpose will be to "enable civilians to utilize flexible tools and tailor programs to the COIN challenges of each specific environment."[23] Though seemingly a sound organizational move, the effectiveness of the SCR will depend on his authority and his relationship with the agencies which will be executing the reconstruction effort in specific provinces and districts, especially those in the military.

CONCLUSION

Starting with the statement of purpose of NSPD 44 which ties reconstruction to promoting "the security of the United States through improved coordination, planning, and implementation" and reinforced in various implementing documents, there is no doubt that reconstruction should be a top priority for the interagency community. But after directing the Secretary of State to "coordinate and lead integrated United States Government efforts"[24] and assigning certain general responsibilities to supporting agencies, the document leaves open some fundamental questions about reconstruction and stabilization, among them the development of an agreed upon interagency approach or concept of reconstruction and the general methods and modalities that it will entail. Any proposal to modify or reform the Army's approach to executing or integrating reconstruction activities in COIN operations will necessarily be undertaken in the context of how these broader issues are approached by the interagency community. Yet it would be unwise for the Army to delay needed changes until the interagency approach is further developed. Certain prudent measures can be taken now that will enhance the Army's overall ability to conduct successful COIN and perhaps set the course for needed interagency reform. A discussion of these measures is the subject of Chapter 6.

ENDNOTES - CHAPTER 5

1. For an analysis of reconstruction in Iraq that underscores this point, see the Special Inspector General for Iraq Reconstruction Report, *Hard Lessons: The Iraq Reconstruction Experience*, Washington, DC: U.S. Government Printing Office, 2009.

2. NSPD-44, unnumbered paragraph entitled "Policy," available from *www.fas.org/irp/offdocs/nspd/nspd-44.html*.

3. Bureau of Political-Military Affairs, *The U.S. Government Counterinsurgency Guide*, Washington, DC: U.S. Department of State, p. 17, available from *www.state.gov/documents/organization/119629.pdf*.

4. Department of Defense Directive (DoDD) 3000.05, Military Support for Stability, Security, Transitions, and Reconstruction, Washington, DC: Department of Defense, November 28, 2005.

5. *Field Manual (FM) 3-0, Operations*, Washington, DC: Department of the Army, June 14, 2001, Figure 3-3.

6. *Field Manual (FM) 3-07, Stability Operations*, Washington, DC: HQ Department of the Army, December 7, 2008, glossary.

7. Conrad Crane and W. Andrew Terrill, *Reconstructing Iraq: Insights, Challenges, and Missions for Military Forces in a Post-Conflict World*, Carlisle, PA: Strategic Studies Institute, U.S. Army War College, February 2003, p. 43.

8. *Ibid*, p. 44.

9. NSPD-44, unnumbered paragraph entitled "Responsibilities of the Department of State—Coordination."

10. NSPD-44, unnumbered paragraph entitled "Coordination Between the Secretary of State and the Secretary of Defense."

11. DoDD 3000.05, paragraph 1.2.

12. DoDD 3000.05, paragraph 4.3.

13. Barton's paper is available from *csis.org/publication/measuring-progress-international-state-building-and-reconstruction*.

14. These observations can be found in any of the quarterly reports issued by SIGIR and SIGAR.

15. The quote is taken from the Department of State S/CRS website, available from *www.state.gov/s/crs*.

16. DoDD 3000-05.

17. For a description of the Civilian Response Corps, see the S/CRS web site, "Introduction to the Civilian Response Corps," available from *www.state.gov/s/crs/about/index.htm#mission*.

18. The diagram is found in MACV 10-12, available from *www.mtholyoke.edu/acad/intrel/pentagon2/pent12.htm*.

19. For an article on the Joint Planning Committee, see Jeff Triestman, "Essential Services as a Counterinsurgency Strategy," *Joint Forces Quarterly*, Issue 53, 2d Quarter, 2009, especially pp. 111-113.

20. *Provincial Reconstruction Team (PRT) Playbook*, Fort Leavenworth, KS: U.S. Army Center for Lessons Learned. The purpose statement is in the second paragraph of Chapter 2. The organization chart is Figure B-3 of the Playbook.

21. *Ibid.*, para. 3.

22. Kabul Cable 00002102, SUBJECT: "Creation of Senior Civilian Representatives in Afghanistan," July 29, 2009.

23. *Ibid.*

24. NSPD-44, unnumbered para. entitled "Responsibilities of the Department of State- Coordination."

CHAPTER 6

ENHANCING ARMY CAPABILITIES FOR RECONSTRUCTION IN COUNTERINSURGENCY

The Army has embraced counterinsurgency theory and doctrine, and the important role that reconstruction plays therein, with gusto. But where some success has been achieved in counterinsurgency (COIN) in ongoing operations, among the various explanations that have been offered for that success, the reconstruction effort hardly figures at all. Attacks to dismantle terrorist and insurgent networks; the ability to secure and protect the population, especially in the urban centers; successful reconciliation efforts—these are what are most often cited as factors that have been critical to winning COIN campaigns. Rarely does anyone hear about a reconstruction effort being part of the reason for success in any COIN campaign. On the contrary, several notable military leaders have observed the failure of the Army to adapt to the full range of requirements—especially the nonlethal ones—required for success on the COIN battlefield. For example, General Peter Chiarelli wrote of his experiences in Baghdad in 2003:

> From an organizational perspective, the Army has successfully created the most modern, effective set of systems for rapid execution of combat operations on the planet. We can achieve immediate effects through command and control of our organic systems. What we have not been able to do is create the systems and processes to execute the nonlethal side as effortlessly as combat operations. Our own regulations, bureaucratic processes, staff relationships, and culture complicate

the ability of our soldiers and leaders to achieve synchronized nonlethal effects across the battlespace. Our traditional training model, still shuddering from the echo of our Cold War mentality, has infused our organization to think in only kinetic terms. This demands new modalities of thinking and a renewed sense of importance to the education of our officer corps.[1]

Assuming that we believe our doctrine and value the lessons of history and the thought of eminent theorists and practitioners of COIN, it will be important for the Army to look for ways to make reconstruction a more effective component of COIN operations — to increase the likelihood of successful campaigns and to reduce some of the toll that COIN is taking on our service members. There are some fundamental reforms that must be considered that could add significantly to Army capabilities to conduct reconstruction. Some of these involve the interagency reforms that were touched upon in Chapter 5 — the most important being a shared understanding of a reconstruction concept across agencies, roles and responsibilities that are more appropriately assigned to and accepted by them, and an enhanced operational focus in those agencies which are instrumental to reconstruction that would allow them to deploy in greater numbers earlier in a campaign. The Army must look hard at its capabilities to participate as a key partner in the interagency effort, and to act alone when that seems appropriate or necessary. The Army could take steps to improve its capabilities to conduct reconstruction in the following areas:

- Improve preparation for reconstruction in COIN.
- Build more capability in Army units to execute key reconstruction tasks.

- Improve the Army's ability to set conditions for the success of interagency partners.

PREPARATION

The interagency community has shown time and again a remarkable lack of preparedness to conduct integrated activities of any type, reconstruction included. In recognition of this weakness, military commanders have established interagency task forces at each combatant command (COCOM) to develop various contingency plans that include consideration of all lines of operation.[2] Though the exact nature and details of these contingency plans are classified, it seems reasonable to assume that such organizations are taking steps to assist in preparing forces (mostly Army and Marine forces) for contingencies in which a COIN operation is likely.

Reconstruction Preparation of the Battlefield.

This preparation should proceed from some sort of reconstruction annex to the overall COIN campaign plan. All appropriate agencies should contribute to writing the annex, and it should serve as a useful guide for designating responsibilities, objectives, timelines, and assessments *ex ante*. An analog to the Army's highly successful process known as "intelligence preparation of the battlefield" might provide a useful baseline for the preparation of this annex.[3]

The annex should include as much information and data as possible about the infrastructure in an area or country as it currently exists — water, electricity, and sewage — for major cities and for national systems, and the locations and state of maintenance of key nodes, facilities, and major lines. Accurate descriptions of key national institutions that will likely become the object of capacity building attempts, such as the judicial system and the state of law enforcement, will be a critical part of the annex. Economic information would allow planning for development efforts that might later become a component of the reconstruction plan. Religious and cultural sites could be identified and added to the plan which might later afford a military force an opportunity to leverage the understanding of these to the advantage of the counterinsurgency effort.

The reconstruction preparation of the battlefield might also include a surveillance plan that assigns reconstruction survey objectives—information needs that should be filled as a first order of priority in the reconstruction process and can be assigned to early entry forces. Reconstruction agencies will have specific information requirements that are often either unknown or insufficiently specified to U.S. forces as they initiate operations in a COIN environment. Assigning requests for information to reconnaissance elements (perhaps with augmentees from various agencies responsible for reconstruction who are embedded with the first arriving units) could be an important step in meeting these needs.

Training.

Beyond some limited training of PRTs that is being conducted by the Army, there is essentially no integrated interagency training of the personnel from the various agencies that will take part in reconstruction activities in support of COIN. Notably lacking is any training of the key officials who will perform management duties at the operational or theater level to ensure that the overall effort is coordinated and appropriately integrated with other operations that are ongoing in support of the COIN campaign plan. When Army headquarters are preparing for deployments to COIN theaters they have virtually no opportunity to work with any representatives from the interagency community with whom they will work to implement reconstruction projects and programs. With the exception of the occasional advisor who turns up to present a seminar on how to work with the interagency community or interjects a helpful comment in that regard during the course of a mission rehearsal exercise or a Battle Command Training Program event, civilian reconstruction experts are largely absent from Army training.

The Army has requested more realistic participation from the interagency community in exercises like this, but has yet to make such participation a priority. Until it does, the training of those who will manage the reconstruction component of a COIN campaign will remain suboptimal.

Preparation at the tactical level has been somewhat better, but still requires improvement. PRTs are the primary interagency entities that are charged with executing reconstruction at the tactical level. Currently the Army has undertaken the training of PRTs that are deploying to Afghanistan as a mission; U.S. Army Forces Command is executing that training. Though the training regimen is relatively thorough for military PRT members, civilian members of the team only participate in a short portion of the overall program, and many training seats dedicated to civilian officials go unfilled. As regards the PRTs deploying to Iraq, there is currently no interagency training to speak of.[4]

Finally, the Army should do a careful review of unit training of military units at home to ensure that they are prepared for reconstruction activities. DoD directives and Army doctrine indicate that Army soldiers and leaders need to be prepared for a wide range of reconstruction tasks, but there is currently no training doctrine that can serve as a basis for a training program to prepare tactical units to perform those tasks. Combat task training is done in accordance with prescribed sets of tasks, conditions, and standards that guide commanders who are preparing their units for deployment. No analogous approach for reconstruction is possible given the dearth of published material on reconstruction that is either distributed or sanctioned by the Army's Training and Doctrine Command.

ADDING RECONSTRUCTION CAPABILITIES TO DEPLOYING ARMY UNITS

To even consider adding reconstruction related capabilities to Army units, the first step will be to decide which reconstruction tasks Army units will really be expected to tackle. DoDD 3000.05 and current Army doctrine notwithstanding, it is not realistic to expect that Army units need to be ready for any of the full range of these tasks. Results of the tabletop exercise described in Chapter 4 track closely with the Army's recent experiences in COIN operations: Upon their arrival in new areas of operation units find themselves dealing with a population that generally has a discrete set of immediate needs that units are currently ill prepared to address. In some cases, resourceful commanders using ingenious ideas have hit upon adequate solutions to some of these needs. In other cases, military leaders conclude that the problems go beyond their ability to handle, and action is deferred until the appropriate civilian agency is able to assist, which is generally not soon enough to have the desired effect in the time frame when solutions could be most useful.

Capabilities Required.

Numerous descriptions of COIN warfare describe the importance of seizing the opportunities presented in the initial stages of the operation to gain support of the population by attending to their most basic and pressing needs. This is especially important if the insurgency threat develops in the wake of a larger conflict. Adding some key capabilities that are either imbedded in the military units that are early deployers or readily available to them as they begin COIN operations could aid them immediately and in the longer term in their efforts to marginalize the influence and reduce the appeal of the insurgency.

Lessons learned and the accounts of experienced practitioners in recent COIN operations, such as those who participated in the tabletop exercise described in Chapter 4, generally indicate that once security has been established in a region, neighborhood, or village, many of the most immediate needs of the people might be addressed in the near term by units with the capability to provide the following:

- Electric power that could be generated at several locations simultaneously or distributed from a central source to several locations.
- Supplies of clean drinking water or water purification capability.

- Equipment and materials to do small scale construction, excavation, digging, and repair to damaged buildings, homes, or other structures.
- Medical teams with access to medicines and supplies and the expertise that is relevant to local health issues.
- Expertise in local government, public administration, and jobs programs who can assist with getting these activities started or back in place.
- Basic development assistance matched to the nature of the local economy, for example, agricultural experts who can provide on the spot help with crops that can be grown and harvested quickly, or veterinary care in rural areas.

Bringing these capabilities to bear in a timely and coordinated fashion has been a real headache for leaders of Army tactical units as they are configured today. Brigade combat team (BCT) commanders that have been faced with these reconstruction challenges have generally had to improvise to find the right types of equipment and personnel with the expertise to assist with these immediate needs. Commanders have purchased generators and distributed them to local townspeople. A commander will look for the soldier (often one of the reservists in the attached Civil Affairs detachment) who has been a city manager, for example, and put him to work assisting local leaders who are tackling tough public administration tasks. Managing the collection and delivery of the kinds of capabilities that can have a quick impact has been handled as an additional duty for some bright captain in the BCT operations center. However, to date, the success stories have most often been the result of individual initiatives, resourced in an ad hoc fashion, and implemented based on the best estimate of effects by relatively junior commanders.

A BCT commander faced with the myriad demands of a COIN operation would benefit greatly from the assistance of a command and control element that is able to organize and integrate the reconstruction component of the overall COIN effort. A reconstruction support organization, properly manned and equipped, with a headquarters that is able to organize and bring to bear the capabilities that are most sought after by the local people and have the highest impact on the COIN operation immediately after the arrival of a counterinsurgent force, could have a decisive impact on a COIN campaign.

Providing the capability to execute a reconstruction effort that can be conducted in a coherent fashion, that is guided by a command and control element responsive to the overall campaign plan and to the tactical commander, and that is supported with capabilities resident in a unit whose mission is reconstruction and is organized and equipped accordingly, would be to take a step in the direction of enabling commanders to accomplish what the Army's doctrine demands. The ability of a local commander to provide relief of this sort on short notice and to sustain it in his area of responsibility could also have a decisive impact on gaining the support of the local population.

Money as a Weapons System.

A special type of capability that is resident in Army units is the funding available to commanders for reconstruction purposes. In COIN operations today, the techniques and procedures involved in identifying the sources of funding, using those funds in an effective and timely manner, and taking the appropriate steps to account for the use of them can be as important as the tactics of a combat operation. Given this fact, it is surprising to see how little has been written officially for commanders about how to use "money as a weapons system."[5]

Commanders have found the funds provided under the auspices of the Commander's Emergency Response Program (CERP) to be especially useful. The CERP provides tactical commanders with the ability to "respond to urgent humanitarian relief and reconstruction projects within their area of responsibility by carrying out programs that will immediately assist the population." CERP provides funds directly to a commander that he can spend for appropriate uses.[6] In most cases, CERP funds can be had much more quickly than some of the other funding made available for reconstruction. Laws and regulations that govern its use also allow for much more discretion at lower levels then comparable monies available to civilian agencies. The CERP has proven to have profound impact on the conduct of COIN.

But the recent use of CERP has raised certain issues that suggest that spending has gone well beyond the original intent for the program. The original idea was to allow commanders to fund smaller, time sensitive, quick impact, high profile projects that could assist in winning the hearts and minds of the local population. Though there are no specific limits on the dollar amounts, the types of projects envisioned were of the variety that would not burden tactical commanders with the requirement to do extensive project management—a capability that does not reside in tactical units. In July 2009 the Special Inspector General for Iraq Reconstruction (SIGIR) released an audit of one of the largest CERP projects in the history of the

Iraq War — a $4.2 million hotel located near the Baghdad Airport. This project was approved by the Multi-National Corps-Iraq (MNC-I) commander, and there are multiple ways that it can be seen as of benefit to at least some portion of the population of Baghdad. But the SIGIR audit does raise the question of whether the CERP program has grown beyond its original intent, and, if so, whether or not the appropriate guidance should be reviewed and changed. There are also numerous construction problems noted in the report that are attributable to inadequate project management. If it is anticipated that CERP will be used to fund projects of this magnitude, then the Army will have to determine how to get appropriate project management capabilities to the commanders who are contracting for large projects such as this one.[7]

There is also a rising tension between the demands of proper oversight as it applies to CERP spending and the initial intent to allow commanders the maximum amount of flexibility possible to get CERP projects initiated. In some units, systems and procedures are so complex and time consuming that much of what was seen as the benefit of the CERP has been lost. On the other end of the spectrum, where units have not applied proper oversight, there have been some notorious cases of fraud, waste, and abuse in the CERP.[8] Recently, public attention has been called to the use of the CERP for purposes that may be in violation of congressional mandates that are tied to the Congress's responsibilities and authority to appropriate specific amounts of money for certain types of reconstruction activities abroad. Quite understandably, Congress views with a jaundiced eye any independent decisions of tactical commanders to use CERP funds that could be interpreted as a means of circumventing congressionally mandated limits.[9]

The CERP was intended to be a short-term program to assist tactical commanders in their efforts to win over the local population in their area of operations. It has proven such a powerful tool in the hands of skillful commanders that Congress has regularly extended the program. It behooves the Army to review the CERP on a regular basis, lest improprieties or abuses cause the cancellation of a truly cost effective "weapons system."

ARMY CAPABILITIES TO SET CONDITIONS FOR THE SUCCESS OF THE CIVILIAN EFFORT

Some might conclude that this area needs no real discussion—that the military need only provide security, and civilian agencies will take care of the rest. But even this topic of providing security for reconstruction activities deserves specific attention. It may be a mistake to simply assume that Army units which are trained for other types of full spectrum operations have prepared for protecting reconstruction activities as a set of "lesser included" tasks. Additionally, there are some very capable systems that the Army already uses as a matter of course that with minor modifications and improvements could be of great assistance to an interagency reconstruction effort, especially since civilian groups currently have nothing comparable at their disposal.

Reconstruction Reconnaissance.

Armed with a list of requests for information from civilian agencies, early entry forces could put some of their reconnaissance elements and assets to work with a specific focus on what it is that the key players in the reconstruction effort will need to know before they arrive. Ideally, civilian agencies would send planners forward with the early entry forces, who could take the answers to these questions and begin an interagency estimate that would be available for use once full teams are able to deploy and the security situation permits them to begin operations.

The proceedings of the tabletop exercise described in Chapter 4 yielded an excellent sense of the types of information needs that civilian agencies will have upon arriving in theater. One of the players representing the U.S. Agency for International Development (USAID) submitted an extensive list of requests for information about factors bearing on reconstruction that might itself serve as a template for early arriving units to use as part of their first reconnaissance missions.[10] Some initial answers to these questions might be available prior to the first entry of deploying forces if a thorough "reconnaissance preparation of the battlefield" of the sort described above were available. "Reconstruction scouts" accompanying early deploying units might only have to update this baseline data to provide as complete and current an estimate as possible to agencies and activities that will follow.

Direct Assistance to Humanitarian Relief Operations.

Though strictly speaking not a reconstruction task, crises involving refugees can have a dramatic impact on reconstruction efforts and on COIN operations. Often units taking part in a military intervention will encounter large movements of refugees who have been uprooted by violence or instability and have taken refuge and sought shelter and sustenance in refugee camps. Army units have at times found it difficult to assist in solving the problems associated with these camps because of the magnitude of the effort involved and because many of the nongovernmental or international relief organizations refuse to cooperate with military forces. But large movements of refugees create a significant destabilizing effect and the refugee camps may become breeding grounds for insurgent activities.

Of course, the preferred method of addressing the flow of refugees is to address the conditions that are causing them to flee in the first place. A successful COIN operation that includes a focused, skillful reconstruction component can go a long way toward achieving that end. But having a plan and maintaining a capability to address a refugee crisis prior to a military intervention seems prudent for virtually any conceivable scenario for regions where an insurgency threatens. This plan might include preexisting arrangements and agreements with other agencies whose mission set includes response to humanitarian crises, even if these arrangements can only be brokered through third parties.[11] Such arrangements would be useful to determine what types of support to a relief effort should be planned. Stocks of relief supplies and equipment that are required to support these plans should be assembled and maintained so that they are ready for deployment in accordance with the agreements that have been made between the combatant command and its service components.

Currently, there are legal restrictions in place that limit the ability of commanders to provide relief that is paid for with appropriated funds unless specific authorization for such assistance is written into the language of the appropriations legislation.

Field Manual (FM) 3-24, Counterinsurgency, cautions that using U.S. Government supplies and equipment for humanitarian relief purposes is subject to requirements for significant coordination with and approvals from the Departments of Defense and State.[12] Part of the preparation for COIN missions might include the accomplishment of as much of this coordination and receiving as many of those permissions as allowable prior to a deployment.

Systems to Manage Reconstruction in COIN — Situational Awareness.

The Army Battle Command System (ABCS) has revolutionized the way that military units gain and maintain situational awareness and has greatly assisted commanders at all levels to make better informed decisions. The ABCS gives commanders a near real time picture of the location and status of virtually every combat system on the battlefield. This has brought an order of magnitude increase in the ability to integrate the effects of various battlefield systems. Given its importance to a COIN operation, it is time to include key information about reconstruction activities into the integrated picture of the battlefield, to ensure situational awareness and provide support to decisionmaking.

First, there is a need to maintain a base line of information that is relevant to reconstruction for nations and regions where there is a contingency plan for a COIN operation, or for any other contingency that might require a reconstruction effort. This baseline data will be critical at the national or theater level and also at the local level as commanders establish their areas of responsibility (AORs) and, in conjunction with civilian agencies, begin their reconstruction projects and programs in support of the COIN campaign. During the conduct of operations, it will be necessary to maintain an accurate and updated common operating picture of the work that is being done by the counterinsurgent force and the host nation to address the various needs of the population. An automated reconstruction management system should be developed that allows organizations and agencies to post and access information about all projects and programs that are being undertaken—locations, status, timelines, and other critical data. Maintaining this data as part of the suite of battle command systems that are currently available in military command posts will assist in efforts to integrate the effects of reconstruction with other types of operations and activities that make up the larger campaign. Naturally, the utility of such a system will depend on the number of agencies and organizations which are willing to post their reconstruction information to the data base. The Army should take the lead on the effort to develop the reconstruction management system, develop means by which other agencies involved in reconstruction can gain access to it, and set the protocols so that other agencies can make their contributions to keeping the common operating picture current.[13]

Systems to Manage Reconstruction in COIN — Decision Support.

Decisions such as those on the type and location of a reconstruction project or program in a COIN campaign generally depend on a number of variables — where the greatest impact can be achieved in terms of improved performance, output, or capacity; receptivity and desired effects on the population who will benefit from the effort; considerations as to the balance of the benefit to various sectors within the population, be they ethnic groups, tribes, or other types of communities; cost of the program or project; and numerous other considerations. Commanders at the operational and tactical level have often found themselves lacking a method of analyzing multiple variables that bear upon a decision that they must make about a particular project or program. As a result, critical decisions about reconstruction are often made in a partially informed fashion, based on one or two of the most obvious variables, without consideration of promising alternatives or any analysis of the full range of effects that are likely to result.

This situation could be addressed if the Army were to develop a decision support program specifically designed to assist with reconstruction decisions. Such a program could be designed around a set of considerations that should be accounted for by a commander in a particular COIN environment, which could be the basis of a series of successive iterations. Using an electrical system that brings power to a district in a commander's area of responsibility as an example, the first iteration of such a program might tell the commander which electrical projects should be undertaken to bring the maximum benefit to the most neighborhoods while still getting power to, say, a central market place. The second iteration might answer the same questions, and bring in another consideration that the commander deems important, for example, maintaining an equitable distribution of electricity between neighborhoods in the district based on ethnicity or tribal makeup. Successive iterations might bring in more nuanced factors about desired effects that could possibly be based on survey data. For example, the answer to a question such as "which neighborhoods rank electricity as the number one quality of life factor and how can we get the most power there with minimal reductions elsewhere?" could affect a commander's decision on which projects to undertake. Answers to such questions might support decisions about providing service to areas where the population is most (or least) inclined to support the COIN.

As with all battle command systems, this type of support to reconstruction decisions depends on sufficient, accurate data of the right type, and can never substitute for the part of decisionmaking that derives from the art of command and the commander's instincts drawn from his personal assessments. But given the complexities involved with reconstruction in COIN and the difficult choices that relatively inexperienced commanders must make in this environment, it seems useful to consider some form of decision support that allows for more thorough analysis and comparison of alternative approaches in the limited time that is usually available to make these decisions.

Tactics for Combined Reconstruction Operations.

Once operating in an environment where multiple agencies are present in the same battle space, military forces are allocated to secure reconstruction efforts as they are available, given other security and COIN operational requirements that must be met. Civilian agencies repeatedly cite security as being the most important requirement that the military must fulfill before they can operate. The only other means available to civilian agencies to secure their reconstruction activities is provided by civilian security contractors who are expensive and have a poor record of conducting their operations in a manner that is consistent with the basic principles of COIN. Thus military commanders often must consider security missions for reconstruction activities as having a high priority among the multiple demands for forces that are placed upon them in COIN.

But military units rarely have the opportunity to prepare or train with civilian agencies to understand their standard procedures for operations in these types of missions. So when called upon to provide security for a reconstruction mission, they have a natural tendency to default to conducting security operations the way they have trained for combat operations in a purely military environment at home station. This may or may not be appropriate to the needs of the civilian reconstruction team operating with the unit. An example of the type of mission that can cause problems is the military convoy that includes a civilian reconstruction team. Small unit tactics generally dictate that, upon receiving fire, the unit returns fire immediately to gain fire superiority and then maneuvers to destroy the threat. Clearly, if the mission is to secure the reconstruction team, there are other considerations that must be taken into account when reacting to contact in a situation like this.

Any action that the Army takes in a COIN operation that enhances the ability to provide security to civilian agencies, and in turn allows them to focus on the timely and effective accomplishment of tasks that will address basic human needs, restoration of services, development, and building capacity in local institutions should be viewed favorably by all involved in the campaign. The first step might be to establish an integrated concept of operations for civilian and military players involved in COIN—a recognized scheme of reconstruction that specifies some standard approaches to the delivery of reconstruction benefits to a local population. Such a scheme might be described as a visualization of how civilian agencies generally prefer to operate and the small unit tactics that can best be employed to support these civilian activities.

A recent RAND study delves into this notion of conducting reconstruction under fire at the local level and proposes some sample operational patterns that could be a start point for the development of a scheme of reconstruction. This sort of common framework would increase familiarity between agencies about their respective ways of doing business (which is uneven among Army units and commanders), support the development of a common taxonomy (which currently does not exist), allow for more focused training of COIN forces (unit training of reconstruction operations rarely occurs), facilitate the ability of military commanders to establish priorities, and allow for smarter and more efficient choices when it comes to allocating forces and resources in COIN.[14]

Provincial Reconstruction Teams.

As previously described, provincial reconstruction teams are small, interagency teams that have been established to support COIN in both Afghanistan and Iraq. The size of PRT's varies from location to location, ranging anywhere from 10 members to over 100. PRT's in Afghanistan are commanded by military officers; those in Iraq have Department of State leadership. Agencies represented in PRT's vary from one to the next, but all generally have a core consisting of military, Department of State, and USAID members.

The mission of the PRTs has been articulated several times by different agencies, never exactly in the same way, and rarely in official documents. The fact is that currently PRTs use the mission statement only as a rough guide to their activities and many interpret their mission in different ways. For the most part, they develop their own priorities and work plans and do their own assessments of their performance and the progress that they are making.

Multiple agencies providing the people to man the PRTs have assessed the worth of the program and the challenges that they have faced.[15] But the most pressing problems are all related to one factor — no department or agency owns the PRT program. As a result, there is no approved doctrine or operational guidance for PRTs except that which is developed in theater, no coherent training program to prepare teams or their members to operate as part of a PRT, and a makeshift method of resourcing them that has been found to be wholly inadequate by PRT commanders and key leaders.

Despite these issues, the potential for PRTs to make a major contribution to a coherent, integrated reconstruction effort at the local level is significant — they are the only interagency operational entity charged with coordinating and executing the reconstruction effort of the multiple agencies at a local level that work in parallel with the efforts of military commanders operating in the same area.

The most important step that the Army could take to help PRTs realize their potential would be to take ownership of the program. Securing proponency would allow the Army to shape PRT missions and organizations in such a way that they could better support the overall COIN effort. The Army could develop doctrine for PRTs, coordinate the conduct of the full course of training and preparation for teams and members, support their deployment, and ensure sufficient resources are made available. The Army may wish to consider building the program around the embedded PRT (or ePRT) which has been a concept employed in Iraq and was judged as extremely successful by commanders there. ePRTs are composed of members from multiple agencies, but instead of operating from a separate location, they live and work directly with tactical commanders, greatly facilitating the coordination of an interagency reconstruction effort at the tactical level.

CONCLUSION

Critics will object to the forgoing recommendations, citing the need for the Army to "stick to warfighting" and not get entangled with "nation-building." Certainly, for several reasons, it would be a mistake for the Army to take steps that would lead to attempting to take on broad capacity and institution building tasks. First, it takes away from the military's ability to set the security conditions that are critical to the success of the overall reconstruction effort. Second, the military lacks the corporate expertise to provide useful advice and assistance in these areas and will never be able to develop the types of relevant skills that are resident in civilian agencies. Third, in cases where the military faces the tradeoff between the near-term benefits of winning hearts and minds by delivering for the people and the longer-term type of capacity building that will eventually lead to the host nation government's ability to address some of their own fundamental problems, military leaders have tended to defer to the near-term efforts, at times at the expense of the overall capacity building effort.

Wide-ranging though they may be, the above recommendations are based on a conceptualization of a strictly defined role for the Army, developed in this monograph, which would take place within a well-coordinated and well-executed whole of government reconstruction effort in support of COIN. As discussed, there is a limit to how much of the reconstruction load we should expect an Army unit to shoulder itself. But there is no limit to the stake that Army forces have in the benefits that can accrue from successful reconstruction in COIN.

ENDNOTES - CHAPTER 6

1. Peter W. Chiarelli and Patrick R. Michaelis, "Winning the Peace: The Requirement for Full Spectrum Operations," *Military Review*, July/August, 2005, p. 15.

2. For a discussion of the interagency task forces, see Terry R. Sopher, "Joint Interagency Coordination Groups (JIACG's): A Temporary Solution to a Long Term Requirement," Carlisle, PA: U.S. Army War College, 2004, available from *www.dtic.mil/cgi-bin/GetTRDoc?AD=ADA423755&Location=U2&doc=GetTRDoc.pdf*.

3. Intelligence Preparation of the Battlefield is described in *Field Manual (FM) 34-130, Intelligence Preparation of the Battlefield*, Washington, DC: Department of the Army, July 1944.

4. Russel L. Honore and David V. Boslego, "Forging Provincial Reconstruction Teams," *Joint Forces Quarterly*, Issue 44, 1st Quarter, 2007.

5. Currently, the Multi-National Corps, Iraq (MNC-I) standard operating procedures document entitled "Money as a Weapons System (MAAWS)," MNC-I, J8, 2007, from which the Center for Army Lessons Learned (CALL) has developed a Lessons Learned manual, is the most comprehensive and specific document covering this topic.

6. *Ibid.* p. 9.

7. SIGIR Audit, "Commanders Emergency Response Program: Hotel Construction Completed, But Project Management Issues Remain," July 26, 2009, available from *www.sigir.mil/*.

8. Jason Sherman, "After 'Rush to Spend' Hundreds of Millions, Lawmakers Scrutinize CERP," *InsideDefense.com*, July 25, 2009.

9. Mark S. Martins, "The Commanders Emergency Response Program," *Joint Forces Quarterly*, Issue 37, 2d Quarter, 2005, available from *www.dtic.mil/doctrine/jel/jfq_pubs/0937.pdf*.

10. As part of her contribution to the Tabletop Exercise, Ms. Elena Brineman, a foreign service officer with extensive experience in USAID and now serving in the U.S. Army's Peacekeeping and Stability Operations Institute at the U.S. Army War College, provided an extensive list of questions that a USAID team would want to have answered prior to their arrival in country. Answers to these questions would provide information on the full range of conditions relevant to successful reconstruction operations in support of a counterinsurgency campaign.

11. For example, Brigadier General Frank Wiercinski, while serving as the Deputy Commanding General of MultiNational Division-North in Iraq from 2006-07, maintained close contact with several IOs and NGOs by working through USAID.

12. *Field Manual (FM) 3-24, Counterinsurgency*, Appendix D, "Legal Considerations," Washington, DC: U.S. Department of the Army.

13. The Department of State's Iraq Reconstruction Management Office maintained an automated system to track the reconstruction effort, known as the Iraq Reconstruction Management System (IRMS). IRMS was notoriously difficult to keep up to date, and access to the data base was extremely limited. As such, it was of little practical use to tactical units.

14. David C. Gompert, Terrence K. Kelly, Brooke Steams Lawson, Michelle Parker, and Kimberly Colloton, *Reconstruction Under Fire: Unifying Civil and Military Counterinsurgency*, Santa Monica, CA: RAND, 2009, presents models for the practice of "civil COIN" for civilian agencies participating in reconstruction and several models or "modes" for tactical units whose mission it is to provide security for reconstruction activities.

15. *Ibid.*

CHAPTER 7

CONCLUSIONS

Even under the best circumstances, reconstruction in counterinsurgency (COIN) is a difficult endeavor. The most critical tasks are numerous and complex. Many participating agencies must undertake missions that fall well out of their existing core competencies or operate in environments that are completely unfamiliar to them. The involvement of multiple agencies which are not accustomed to working together makes coordination difficult. And all of this must take place in an environment where an armed, violent foe who understands the disadvantage to him of a successful reconstruction effort, is determined to go to almost any length to resist progress or destroy what has been accomplished.

In an assessment of an ongoing COIN operation, General David H. Petraeus observed that "hard is not hopeless."[1] Extending his logic, it can be said that reconstruction in COIN is hard, but it becomes less hopeless if the counterinsurgent understands what needs to be accomplished and to what end, and he has a plan and can mount a coordinated effort to execute that plan. Chapter 1 of *Field Manual (FM) 3-24, Counterinsurgency*, concludes with the introduction of some "paradoxes of COIN" that are designed "to stimulate thinking, not to limit it." Herewith in order to stimulate thinking and make hard less hopeless are some paradoxes of reconstruction.

In Coin, Time is on the Side of the Insurgent, but Reconstruction Takes Time.

COIN forces place a premium on quick results and actions that will produce effects before the grip of the insurgency can take hold on the population. Reconstruction activities, especially those that are designed to build capacity in host nation institutions, are generally time intensive. The need to show some progress in short order can, at times, overwhelm the strategic patience that is required to fully implement projects and programs that can bring lasting reform.

Reconstruction Requires Security, But Reconstruction Is an Important Precondition to Addressing Security Problems in a Given Battle Space.

Military commanders, especially, will perceive reconstruction as a key factor in influencing the populace to support the COIN, gain cooperation, and separate the guerrilla from the population. Therefore, they will push for reconstruction projects as early as possible to assist with their efforts to win over the population and establish security. Civilian agencies that have not trained or prepared their personnel to work in a combat environment will quite naturally push for the best security conditions possible before initiating any major reconstruction efforts.

If You Build It, They Will Come.

Reconstruction creates additional security requirements. A promising project presents a great information operations opportunity for the counterinsurgent to show the benefits of cooperation. But it also creates a target for the insurgent that he otherwise would not have had—an opportunity to undermine the credibility and the legitimacy of the counterinsurgent and the host nation.

Reconstruction Raises Expectations, Which Sometimes Means that They Have Farther to Fall.

Once it becomes known that the United States has taken on the tasks associated with improving the way of life of the population, expectations rise quickly. And when raised in this manner, expectations never recede; who can believe that a nation that "put a man on the moon" would be unable to sustain the delivery of essential services to a handful of families? And unmet expectations are the grist of dissatisfaction on which the guerrilla thrives.

Reconstruction Breeds Dependency in the Host Nation, and Dependency Has a Corrosive Effect on Legitimacy, Which Is the Main Objective of Counterinsurgency.

Even if limited to a short period of time, providing the type of assistance that is delivered to a host nation as part of a holistic reconstruction program during a COIN operation runs the risk of creating a dependency in the government that the counterinsurgent is attempting to assist, especially if that government is weak to begin with. This dependency can be used by the insurgent as a weapon to assist in making the case that the host nation government is ineffectual, undependable, and reliant on the assistance of outsiders to perform even the most routine functions of government.

Effective Reconstruction Empowers and Brings Legitimacy—Sometimes to the Wrong Leaders.

Bias or corruption in government can often be used by the insurgent as an accelerant or a means to gain legitimacy for his cause. If the benefits of reconstruction are viewed by the population as propping up a corrupt or criminal leader, the counterinsurgent stands to lose. Additionally, it is often the case that the benefits of reconstruction in an area that is poorly or corruptly governed or administered never trickle down to the people, which will do no good and perhaps cause great harm to the efforts of the counterinsurgent.

Drawing directly from FM 3-24: "Some of the best weapons for counterinsurgents do not shoot."

The narrative that expands on this paradox in FM 3-24 centers on a discussion of "the lasting victory that comes from a vibrant economy, political participation, and restored hope,"[2] and sums up in a concise and catchy way many of the main points related to reconstruction that appear in current Army doctrine.

Of course, the unspoken corollary to this paradox is: Even as a weapon that does not shoot, reconstruction can end up being dangerous to the hunter as well as the hunted. The counterinsurgent's ultimate objectives are a manageable security environment and strong national institutions that have the confidence and the support of the people. A coordinated, skillfully executed reconstruction program is essential to those ends. But reconstruction that is mismanaged, bungled, and obviously ineffectual not only represents a lost opportunity to advance the cause; it also may well put a weapon in the hands of the insurgent.

ENDNOTES - CHAPTER 7

1. See, for example, Geneeral David Petraeus, quoted by Josh Partlow in "Path in Iraq Hard But Not Hopeless, US General Says," *The Washington Post*, February 11, 2007.

2. *Field Manual (FM) 3-24, Counterinsurgency*, Washington, DC: HQ Department of the Army, June 2006, para. 1-153.